The Best of **Mr. Food**®

Dinner on the Double

❝When your mission is for meals in minutes, look here for quick, easy, and do-able recipes for even the busiest of families.❞

Santa Fe Pizza,
page 117

Flank Steak with Tomato-Olive Relish, page 98

Double Chocolate Toffee
Brownies, page 198

The Best of Mr. Food®

Dinner on the Double

Oxmoor House®

©2005 by Oxmoor House, Inc.
Book Division of Southern Progress Corporation
P.O. Box 2262, Birmingham, Alabama 35201-2262

ISBN: 0-8487-2894-7
ISSN: 1534-5505
Library of Congress Control Number: 2005925530

Printed in the United States of America
Third Printing 2006

Mr. Food® and OOH IT'S SO GOOD!! are registered marks owned by Ginsburg Enterprises Incorporated.

Ginsburg Enterprises Incorporated
   Chief Executive Officer: Art Ginsburg
   Chief Operating Officer: Steven Ginsburg
   Vice President, Creative Business Development: Howard Rosenthal
   Vice President, Publishing: Caryl Ginsburg Fantel
   Vice President, Sales and Licensing: Thomas R. Palombo
   Director of Finance and Administration: Nanette Todd

Oxmoor House, Inc.
   Editor in Chief: Nancy Fitzpatrick Wyatt
   Executive Editor: Susan Carlisle Payne
   Art Director: Cynthia Rose Cooper
   Copy Chief: Allison Long Lowery

THE BEST OF MR. FOOD® DINNER ON THE DOUBLE, featuring the recipes of Mr. Food, Art Ginsburg
   Editor: Kelly Hooper Troiano
   Assistant Foods Editor: McCharen Pratt
   Copy Editor: Donna Baldone
   Editorial Assistant: Terri Laschober
   Director, Test Kitchens: Elizabeth Tyler Luckett
   Assistant Director, Test Kitchens: Julie Christopher
   Test Kitchens Staff: Kristi Carter, Nicole L. Faber, Kathleen Royal Phillips,
      Elise Weis, Kelley Self Wilton
   Senior Photographer: Jim Bathie
   Photographer: Brit Huckabay
   Senior Photo Stylist: Kay E. Clarke
   Photo Stylist: Amy Wilson
   Director of Production: Phillip Lee
   Production Manager: Greg Amason
   Production Assistant: Faye Porter Bonner
   Publishing Systems Administrator: Rick Tucker

   Contributors:
   Designer: Rita Yerby
   Indexer: Mary Ann Laurens
   Intern: Ashley Lanier
   Photo Stylist: Missie Crawford

To order additional publications, call 1-800-765-6400.

For more books to enrich your life, visit **oxmoorhouse.com**

Cover: *Beef and Bean Chimichangas, page 102*

Contents

Welcome!!

"If you're like most busy people today, you don't have lots of time to spend in the kitchen, but you still want that homemade, made-from-scratch taste. Well, with a few shortcuts, I'll show you how to achieve that goal—fast!

Twelve menus plus a game plan for minimizing your time in the kitchen take the guesswork out of what to have for dinner. The kids will be thumbs up for Pizza and Pasta, and you can keep it simple with the wonders of one-dish meals—there's even a no-cook chapter! Round out your dinner with one of my speedy sides, fuss-free breads, and irresistible desserts. We'll show you how slow-cooking can be fast, and you'll discover the time-savin' convenience of marinating and freezing recipes ahead. Quick and easy is the key. So get cookin', and get dinner to your gang on the double!**"

Mr. Food

Menus in Minutes

"With 12 delicious, quick 'n' easy menus to choose from, you'll never have to ask 'What's for Dinner?' again!"

menu
- Burgers
- Salsa & Chips
- Brownies

Menu

Italian Night
serves 4

Zesty Spaghetti and Meatballs
Greens and Vinaigrette

Zesty Spaghetti and Meatballs

4 servings

prep: 5 minutes   cook: 30 minutes

1 (16-ounce) can tomato sauce
2 cloves garlic, pressed
1 teaspoon sugar
¼ teaspoon dried Italian seasoning
¼ teaspoon crushed red pepper
    (optional)

½ (38-ounce) package frozen cooked
    meatballs
2 teaspoons dried basil
Warm cooked spaghetti

1 Cook first 4 ingredients and, if desired, crushed red pepper in a heavy saucepan over medium-high heat about 10 minutes, stirring occasionally.

2 Stir in meatballs and basil. Reduce heat to low, and cook about 20 minutes or until thoroughly heated, stirring occasionally. Serve over spaghetti.

Pasta Pointers

Fresh pasta cooks in 1 to 3 minutes, while dried pasta takes 6 to 15 minutes. Be sure to toss cooked pasta with a sauce as soon as possible after draining because pasta begins to stick as it cools. Adding a small amount of oil to the boiling water will also prevent pasta from sticking.

Greens and Vinaigrette

4 to 6 servings

prep: 5 minutes

1 clove garlic, minced
1 teaspoon sugar
⅛ teaspoon salt
⅛ teaspoon dry mustard
3 to 4 tablespoons lemon juice

½ cup olive oil
1 (16-ounce) package gourmet salad
 greens

1 Process first 5 ingredients in a blender until smooth, stopping to scrape down sides.

2 Turn blender on high, and add oil in a slow, steady stream. Drizzle over greens.

Game Plan

1. Cook pasta according to package directions.

2. Meanwhile, cook tomato sauce mixture.

3. Add meatballs and basil to sauce.

4. While spaghetti cooks, mix together vinaigrette.

5. Toss together salad greens and vinaigrette, and serve sauce and meatballs over warm cooked pasta.

Menu

Kids Love It!

serves 4

Chicken Strips with Honey Sauce
French fries
Tossed green salad

Chicken Strips with Honey Sauce

4 servings

prep: 15 minutes   cook: 10 minutes

4   boneless chicken breasts

1   large egg
1   tablespoon cornstarch
2   teaspoons soy sauce

½   cup sesame seeds
¼   cup fine, dry breadcrumbs
        (prepared)
1   teaspoon garlic salt
3   tablespoons butter, melted

½   cup Dijon mustard
¼   cup honey
¼   to ½ teaspoon hot sauce

1 Cut chicken into strips.

2 Whisk together egg and next 2 ingredients in a large bowl; add chicken strips, coating well. Let stand 5 minutes.

3 Preheat the broiler. Combine sesame seeds, breadcrumbs, and garlic salt in a large resealable plastic bag. Add chicken, seal bag, and shake to coat. Place chicken on a lightly greased baking sheet; drizzle with butter.

4 Broil 5½" from heat 5 minutes on each side or until golden.

5 Stir together mustard, honey, and hot sauce. Serve with chicken strips.

Game Plan

1. Cook French fries in oven according to package directions.
2. Coat chicken with batter and breadcrumb mixture, and broil.
3. Prepare and toss salad while chicken cooks.

Menu

Mediterranean Quickie
serves 4

Gyro Burgers with Tahini Sauce
Pita chips
Vanilla yogurt with fresh fruit

Gyro Burgers with Tahini Sauce

4 servings

prep: 20 minutes   cook: 12 minutes

¼   cup tahini (see note)
¼   cup water
2   tablespoons lemon juice
¼   teaspoon salt
⅛   teaspoon garlic powder
1   pound extra-lean ground beef
1   teaspoon Greek seasoning

4   pita rounds
4   lettuce leaves
8   large tomato slices
4   thin red onion slices
¼   cup feta cheese

1 Whisk together tahini, water, lemon juice, salt, and garlic powder; set aside. Combine beef and Greek seasoning. Shape into 4 patties.

2 Preheat the grill to medium-high heat (350° to 400°). Grill burgers 5 to 6 minutes on each side or until beef is no longer pink.

3 Cut off 2" of bread from 1 side of each pita round, forming a pocket. Line each pita with 1 lettuce leaf, 2 tomato slices, and 1 red onion slice; add burger. Drizzle each with 2 tablespoons reserved tahini sauce, and sprinkle with 1 tablespoon cheese.

Note: Look for tahini (a thick paste made from crushed sesame seeds that's used as flavoring in Middle Eastern cooking) in the imported foods section of your supermarket or in Mediterranean or Middle Eastern markets.

Game Plan

1. Mix tahini sauce, and shape burger patties.
2. While grill heats, prepare veggies for burgers and fruit for dessert; cover and chill.
3. Grill burgers.
4. Serve up chips, and assemble burgers.

Menu

Sandwich Night
serves 4

Reuben Melts
Deli potato salad
Chocolate-Mint Sundaes

Reuben Melts

4 servings

prep: 15 minutes   cook: 15 minutes

1   cup mayonnaise
¼   cup ketchup
1   to 2 tablespoons sweet pickle relish
⅛   teaspoon ground red pepper

3   cups coleslaw mix

8   rye bread slices
1   (6-ounce) package Swiss cheese
        slices
12   ounces thinly sliced ham

Butter-flavored nonstick cooking spray

1 Preheat the oven to 375°. Stir together first 4 ingredients.

2 Stir together coleslaw mix and ½ cup mayonnaise mixture.

3 Spread 1 tablespoon mayonnaise mixture evenly on 1 side of each bread slice; top 4 slices evenly with cheese, ham, and coleslaw mixture. Top with remaining bread slices.

4 Place sandwiches on a baking sheet coated with butter-flavored nonstick cooking spray. Coat bottom of another baking sheet with cooking spray, and place coated-side down on sandwiches.

5 Bake at 375° for 10 to 15 minutes or until bread is golden and cheese melts.

Chocolate-Mint Sundaes

4 servings

prep: 5 minutes   cook: 1 minute

12   (0.25-ounce) chocolate-covered
         peppermint patties
2   tablespoons milk
Vanilla ice cream

1 Place peppermint patties and milk in a small microwave-safe glass bowl. Cover and microwave at HIGH 1 minute or until patties melt, stirring every 15 seconds. Serve over ice cream.

Game Plan

1. Stir together mayonnaise mixture and coleslaw mixture for sandwiches.

2. Assemble sandwiches, and bake.

3. Spoon up potato salad, and serve with hot sandwiches.

4. Prepare chocolate-mint sauce for dessert, and serve over ice cream.

Menu
Burger Fiesta
serves 6

Stuffed Border Burgers
Tortilla chips
Mocha Latte

Stuffed Border Burgers

6 servings

prep: 20 minutes   cook: 10 minutes

1½   pounds lean ground beef
½   cup finely chopped onion
1   (4.25-ounce) can chopped ripe
       black olives, drained
2   tablespoons ketchup
1   teaspoon chili powder
1   teaspoon fajita seasoning
6   (1-ounce) slices Monterey Jack
       cheese with peppers

½   cup sour cream
⅓   cup ketchup
1   (4.5-ounce) can chopped green
       chilies
1   tablespoon minced fresh cilantro
6   onion rolls, split and toasted
Toppings: shredded lettuce, sliced
       tomatoes, guacamole

1 Preheat the grill to medium-high heat (350° to 400°). Combine first 6 ingredients. Shape mixture into 12 (4") patties. Fold cheese slices into quarters; place cheese on each of 6 patties. Top with remaining 6 patties, pressing to seal edges.

2 Grill burgers, covered, 4 to 5 minutes on each side or until done.

3 Stir together sour cream, ketchup, chilies, and cilantro. Serve burgers on rolls with sauce and desired toppings.

Mocha Latte Syrup

1¼ cups (enough for 20 lattes)

prep: 5 minutes   cook: 1 minute

¾   cup sugar
⅓   cup unsweetened cocoa
¼   cup instant espresso
½   teaspoon ground cinnamon
½   cup water
2   tablespoons vanilla extract

1 Combine sugar, cocoa, espresso, and cinnamon in a medium saucepan. Whisk in ½ cup water, and bring to a boil over medium heat. Boil 1 minute, stirring often. Remove from heat; stir in vanilla. Pour into a jar; cover and refrigerate up to 2 weeks.

2 To make a Mocha Latte beverage, spoon 1 tablespoon Mocha Latte Syrup into a coffee cup; stir in ¾ cup hot milk.

Game Plan

1. Combine beef mixture while grill heats.

2. Stir together sour cream mixture, and prepare toppings while burgers cook.

3. Serve tortilla chips with burgers.

4. Heat milk, and stir into Mocha Latte Syrup for a satisfying after-dinner beverage.

Take a Break
Enjoy the fancy drinks sold in coffee shops in your own home by keeping this syrup in your fridge.

Menu

Coastal Celebration
serves 6

Creamy Shrimp 'n' Pasta
Tossed green salad
Key Lime Pie

Creamy Shrimp 'n' Pasta

6 servings

prep: 15 minutes   cook: 8 minutes

1   (7-ounce) package vermicelli

1   (12-ounce) jar roasted red bell
      peppers, drained

1   (8-ounce) package ⅓-less-fat cream
      cheese, softened

½   cup chicken broth

3   cloves garlic, chopped

½   teaspoon ground red pepper

2   pounds cooked, peeled large fresh
      shrimp

¼   cup chopped fresh basil or
      1 tablespoon dried basil

1 Prepare pasta according to package directions. Keep pasta warm.

2 While pasta cooks, process bell peppers and next 4 ingredients in a blender or food processor until smooth, scraping down sides. Pour mixture into a large skillet. Cook over medium heat 5 minutes, stirring often, until heated.

3 Add shrimp, and cook 2 to 3 minutes or until thoroughly heated, stirring occasionally. Remove from heat. Serve over pasta. Sprinkle with basil.

Shrimp Savvy
To cook your own shrimp, you'll need to buy 4 pounds of unpeeled large fresh shrimp that haven't been cooked.

Key Lime Pie

6 servings

prep: 5 minutes   chill: 2 hours

1   (14-ounce) can sweetened
       condensed milk
½   cup Key lime juice (see note)
1   tablespoon grated Key lime rind
1   (8-ounce) container frozen whipped
       topping, thawed and divided
1   (6-ounce) graham cracker crust

6   thin slices Key lime

1 Combine milk and lime juice in a bowl; stir until blended. Stir in lime rind; gently fold in ¾ cup whipped topping. Pour into crust. Cover and chill at least 2 hours.

2 To serve, top each slice with a dollop of whipped topping and a lime slice.

Note: Fresh Key lime juice will taste better than bottled, but remember to grate the rind before juicing the lime. If Key limes are not available, substitute regular limes.

Game Plan

1. Prepare pie, and chill at least 2 hours.

2. Cook pasta according to package directions.

3. Meanwhile, process pepper mixture, and cook.

4. While sauce cooks, toss salad.

5. Add shrimp to sauce, and continue cooking.

6. Serve shrimp and sauce over warm cooked pasta.

7. Top pie slices with whipped topping and a lime slice.

Menu

Pork Chop Special
serves 6

Spicy Brown Mustard Chops
Store-bought refrigerated roasted potatoes
Italian Green Beans

Spicy Brown Mustard Chops

6 servings

prep: 10 minutes   cook: 6 minutes

½   teaspoon salt
½   teaspoon garlic powder
¼   teaspoon pepper
½   cup spicy brown mustard
6   (½"-thick) boneless pork chops

1   cup all-purpose flour

¼   cup vegetable or canola oil

1 Combine first 3 ingredients. Spread mustard evenly on both sides of pork chops, and sprinkle with salt mixture.

2 Place flour in a shallow dish; dredge chops in flour.

3 Heat oil in a large skillet over medium-high heat. Add chops, and cook 2 to 3 minutes on each side or until golden. Drain on paper towels, and serve immediately.

Which Flavor Do You Favor?
You can vary the flavor of these pork chops by substituting Dijon mustard or coarse-grained mustard for the spicy brown mustard.

Italian Green Beans

6 to 8 servings

prep: 5 minutes   cook: 30 minutes

1   tablespoon butter
1   tablespoon olive oil
1   small onion, chopped

3   (10-ounce) packages frozen Italian-
        style green beans, thawed
1   cup vegetable broth
1   tablespoon chopped fresh basil or
        1 teaspoon dried basil
1   teaspoon salt
½   teaspoon pepper

1 Melt butter with oil in a large skillet over medium heat; add onion, and sauté 5 minutes or until tender.

2 Add green beans and remaining ingredients; cook 20 to 25 minutes or until beans are tender.

Game Plan

1. Begin sautéing onion for green beans.

2. Add green beans and remaining ingredients, and cook until tender.

3. Meanwhile, sprinkle pork chops with seasoning, and dredge in flour.

4. Prepare roasted potatoes according to package directions.

5. Meanwhile, cook pork chops, and serve immediately with green beans and roasted potatoes.

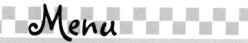

Menu

Asian Night "In"
serves 4

Gingered Beef Stir-fry
Lemon-Scented Sugar Snaps
Fortune Cookies

Gingered Beef Stir-fry

4 servings

prep: 25 minutes   cook: 7 minutes

1   pound sirloin steak, chilled (see tip)
¼   teaspoon salt
½   teaspoon pepper

2   teaspoons vegetable oil
2   tablespoons grated fresh ginger
½   teaspoon minced garlic
1   tablespoon soy sauce

½   cup beef broth
2   teaspoons cornstarch
6   green onions, cut diagonally into
        1" pieces
Warm cooked long-grain rice

1 Cut steak diagonally across the grain into wafer-thin slices. Sprinkle with salt and pepper.

2 Heat oil in a large nonstick skillet over high heat. Add ginger, and sauté 2 minutes or until tan-colored. Add minced garlic, and sauté 30 seconds. Add beef; cook 2 minutes, stirring constantly. Stir in soy sauce.

3 Stir together beef broth and cornstarch until smooth. Drizzle over beef mixture. Cook, stirring constantly, 1 minute or until thickened. Add green onions; cook 1 minute. Serve immediately over rice.

❝Chilling the beef in the freezer for 5 minutes will make it easier for you to cut it into very thin slices. And if you like hot Asian food, add ½ teaspoon crushed red pepper to the beef along with the green onions—that'll snap your taste buds to attention!❞

Lemon-Scented Sugar Snaps

4 to 6 servings

prep: 15 minutes   cook: 10 minutes

2   pounds fresh sugar snap peas

2   tablespoons butter
2   cloves garlic, minced
2   teaspoons grated lemon rind
1   tablespoon lemon juice
¾   teaspoon salt
½   teaspoon freshly ground pepper

1 Cook peas in boiling salted water to cover 5 minutes or until crisp-tender. Drain and plunge into ice water to stop the cooking process; drain.

2 Melt butter in a medium skillet over medium-high heat; add peas, and sauté 3 minutes. Add garlic and remaining ingredients. Sauté 2 minutes or until thoroughly heated.

Note: To boil sugar snap peas ahead, follow step 1; then wrap the peas in paper towels, and place in a resealable plastic bag. Seal and chill up to 8 hours.

Game Plan

1. Cook rice according to package directions.

2. Chill beef in freezer 5 minutes before slicing.

3. Meanwhile, cook sugar snap peas in boiling water.

4. Sauté beef and garlic; stir together beef broth and cornstarch. Drizzle over beef mixture, and continue cooking; add green onions.

5. Sauté sugar snap peas as directed.

6. Serve beef stir-fry over warm cooked rice and with sugar snap peas.

7. Read fortunes, and enjoy cookies!

Menu
Company's Coming
serves 6

Store-bought premarinated pork tenderloin (2 pounds)
Baked potatoes
Smothered Green Beans
Three-Ingredient Chocolate Mousse

Smothered Green Beans

6 servings

prep: 10 minutes   cook: 23 minutes

4	to 6 bacon slices
3	celery ribs, chopped
1	pound fresh green beans, trimmed
1	medium onion, chopped
1	red bell pepper, chopped
3	plum tomatoes, seeded and chopped
2	cloves garlic, minced
1½	teaspoons salt
½	teaspoon dried basil
¼	teaspoon black pepper

1 Cook bacon in a large skillet until crisp; remove bacon, and drain on paper towels, reserving 2 tablespoons drippings in skillet. Crumble bacon, and set aside.

2 Cook celery and next 3 ingredients in hot drippings in skillet over medium-high heat 10 to 12 minutes.

3 Add tomatoes and remaining 4 ingredients; cook 5 minutes or until beans are tender, stirring often. Stir in crumbled bacon.

So-o-o Easy!
The packaged pork tenderloins available in supermarkets make quick, easy entrées. Because they're already marinated, they can go straight from the package to your oven or grill.

Three-Ingredient Chocolate Mousse

6 servings

prep: 10 minutes   cook: 1½ minutes   chill: 2 hours

1   (12-ounce) bag semisweet
        chocolate chips (2 cups)
2½ cups whipping cream, divided
1½ teaspoons vanilla extract

Garnishes: whipped cream, grated
        chocolate

1 Microwave chocolate chips and ½ cup cream in a large microwave-safe glass bowl at HIGH 1½ minutes or until melted, stirring twice. Stir in vanilla, blending well. Cool 5 minutes.

2 Beat remaining 2 cups cream at medium speed of an electric beater until soft peaks form; fold cream into chocolate mixture. Spoon into individual dessert dishes. Garnish, if desired. Cover and chill 2 hours.

Game Plan

1. Prepare chocolate mousse, and chill at least 2 hours.
2. Begin cooking tenderloin according to package directions.
3. Cook bacon, crumble, and set aside.
4. Pierce 6 potatoes with a fork, and microwave at HIGH 20 to 24 minutes or until done.
5. Cook green beans and chopped vegetables in skillet; stir in crumbled bacon.

Menu

Meat Loaf Special
serves 8

Mini Beef-Veggie Loaves
Refrigerated mashed potatoes
Lemony Herbed Broccoli

Mini Beef-Veggie Loaves

8 servings

prep: 20 minutes   cook: 25 minutes

2 pounds ground chuck
2 cups soft breadcrumbs (homemade)
2 large eggs
½ cup chopped onion
¼ cup grated carrot
¼ cup chopped green bell pepper
1 (14.5-ounce) can diced tomatoes, drained
1½ teaspoons salt
1 teaspoon dry mustard
½ teaspoon black pepper

¼ cup ketchup

1 Preheat the oven to 450°. Combine all ingredients except ketchup, mixing well. Shape mixture into 8 mini loaves; place on rack of a lightly greased broiler pan.

2 Bake at 450° for 20 minutes. Spread ketchup evenly over meat loaves; bake 5 more minutes.

Pumped Up Potatoes
Refrigerated mashed potatoes taste great when they're just heated and served. But for additional flavor, try adding butter, shredded cheese, or chopped chives, or all three!

Lemony Herbed Broccoli

8 servings

prep: 4 minutes   cook: 3 minutes

¼   cup butter
2   (10-ounce) packages frozen broccoli
       florets, thawed
2   teaspoons grated lemon rind
2   tablespoons lemon juice
¾   teaspoon salt
½   teaspoon dried basil

1 Melt butter in a large skillet over medium heat. Add broccoli florets and remaining ingredients. Cook 3 minutes or until thoroughly heated, stirring gently.

Game Plan

1. Thaw frozen broccoli.

2. Combine meat loaf mixture, and bake.

3. Meanwhile, cook mashed potatoes in the microwave according to package directions.

4. Stir additional ingredients into potatoes, if desired (see box at left).

5. Cook broccoli mixture in a large skillet.

Menu

Down-Home Dinner
serves 4

Fried Pork Chops with Cream Gravy
Cheddar Scalloped Potatoes
Sautéed Spinach (see box, opposite page)
Store-bought biscuits

Fried Pork Chops with Cream Gravy

4 servings

prep: 7 minutes   cook: 12 minutes

1	teaspoon Cajun seasoning
⅛	teaspoon garlic powder
⅛	teaspoon pepper
4	(4-ounce) boneless center-cut pork chops
½	cup all-purpose flour, divided
¼	cup buttermilk
2	tablespoons vegetable oil
¾	cup milk
⅛	teaspoon salt

1 Combine Cajun seasoning, garlic powder, and pepper. Rub seasoning mixture evenly on both sides of pork chops.

2 Reserve 1 tablespoon flour, and set aside. Place remaining flour in a shallow dish. Dip chops in buttermilk; dredge in flour.

3 Heat oil in a large heavy skillet over medium heat; add chops, and cook 5 minutes on each side or until golden. Drain on paper towels.

4 Reduce heat to medium-low. Whisk reserved 1 tablespoon flour into milk; add salt, and cook in skillet, stirring constantly, until thickened and bubbly. Serve immediately with chops.

Cheddar Scalloped Potatoes

4 servings

prep: 10 minutes   cook: 15 minutes

1   pound baking potatoes, cut into
      ¼"-thick slices
4   green onions, thinly sliced

1½ teaspoons butter
1   tablespoon all-purpose flour
⅛   teaspoon salt
⅛   teaspoon ground red pepper
1   cup milk
½   cup (2 ounces) shredded Cheddar
      cheese

1 Arrange potatoes and green onions in an 8" square microwave-safe baking dish. Cover with heavy-duty plastic wrap, and vent. Microwave at HIGH 10 minutes or until potatoes are tender, stirring every 4 minutes. Set aside.

2 Coat a 2-cup microwave-safe glass measuring cup with nonstick cooking spray; add butter. Microwave at HIGH 30 seconds or until butter melts. Stir in flour, salt, and pepper. Add milk; stir until smooth. Microwave at HIGH 3 minutes or until thickened, stirring halfway through with a wire whisk. Stir in cheese; microwave at HIGH 30 seconds or until cheese melts. Pour over potatoes and onions; stir. Microwave at HIGH 1 minute or until thoroughly heated.

Game Plan

1. Cook potatoes and green onions in microwave for 10 minutes.

2. Meanwhile, combine seasoning mix, and rub on pork chops.

3. Cook pork chops.

4. Begin assembling and cooking cheese sauce in microwave for potatoes while pork chops cook.

5. Prepare sautéed spinach.

6. Pour cheese sauce over potatoes, and microwave until heated.

7. Prepare gravy for pork chops, and serve immediately.

Sautéed Spinach

Sauté 2 cloves of garlic, minced, in butter for 30 seconds. Add 2 (10-ounce) packages of fresh spinach, ¼ teaspoon crushed red pepper, and 2 tablespoons lemon juice. Sauté 3 to 4 minutes or until spinach wilts, and serve.

Menu

Soup 'n' Salad Supper

serves 4 to 6

Tortilla Soup
Iceberg lettuce wedges with Ranch-style dressing
Vanilla ice cream and caramel sauce

Tortilla Soup

6 cups

prep: 5 minutes   cook: 30 minutes

2   (14-ounce) cans chicken broth
1   (14½-ounce) can Cajun-style
        stewed tomatoes
3   tablespoons lemon juice
3   cloves garlic, pressed
2   teaspoons chili powder
¼   teaspoon ground red pepper

1½ cups chopped cooked chicken
1   cup frozen corn kernels
1   (15-ounce) can black beans, rinsed
        and drained
2   tablespoons half-and-half
1   green onion, thinly sliced
Tortilla chips
Shredded Mexican four-cheese blend
        (optional)

1 Bring first 6 ingredients to a boil in a Dutch oven.

2 Reduce heat; add chicken and next 4 ingredients, and simmer 20 minutes. Serve with tortilla chips and, if desired, cheese.

Game Plan

1. Assemble and simmer soup according to recipe directions.
2. Rinse lettuce, and cut into wedges while soup simmers.
3. Serve soup with tortilla chips and cheese, and drizzle Ranch dressing over lettuce wedges.
4. Heat store-bought caramel sauce according to instructions on jar, and drizzle over ice cream.

One-Dish Wonders

❝When you're short on time, one-dish meals are the perfect solution to your mealtime dilemma. They're quick, they're easy—they're all you need in one dish.❞

Veggie Scramble

4 servings

prep: 10 minutes   cook: 10 minutes

½	small red bell pepper
½	small green bell pepper
¼	small sweet onion
1	tablespoon olive oil
8	large eggs, lightly beaten
¼	teaspoon salt
½	teaspoon freshly ground black pepper
½	cup (2 ounces) shredded sharp Cheddar cheese

1 Chop bell peppers and onion. Heat olive oil in a large skillet over medium-high heat. Add vegetables, and cook 5 minutes or until tender.

2 Whisk together eggs, salt, and black pepper. Add mixture to vegetables in skillet, and cook, without stirring, until eggs begin to set on bottom. Draw a spatula across bottom of skillet to form large curds. Sprinkle with cheese, and continue cooking until eggs are thickened but still moist. (Do not stir constantly.) Remove from heat. Serve immediately.

Super Good
These veggie-filled eggs are super fast and fresh. Serve 'em with whole grain toast for a meal that's super healthy!

Vegetable Quesadillas

2 servings

prep: 10 minutes   cook: 15 minutes

2   tablespoons olive oil
1   cup sliced fresh or frozen yellow
     squash, thawed
½   cup sliced fresh mushrooms
½   cup chopped onion
½   teaspoon salt
¼   teaspoon pepper
½   teaspoon hot sauce

1   cup (4 ounces) shredded
     mozzarella cheese
2   (8") flour tortillas

Salsa

1 Heat oil in a large skillet over medium-high heat. Add squash and next 5 ingredients, and sauté until vegetables are crisp-tender; remove vegetables from skillet, reserving oil in skillet.

2 Place ¼ cup mozzarella cheese on half of each tortilla; top evenly with vegetable mixture and remaining ½ cup cheese. Fold tortillas over filling.

3 Cook quesadillas in reserved hot oil in skillet over medium heat 3 to 5 minutes on each side or until light golden. Serve immediately with salsa.

66No one will ask, 'Where's the beef?' when they bite into these quesadillas that are stuffed with fresh squash and mushrooms and loaded with gooey cheese.99

Breakfast Pizza

4 to 6 servings

prep: 8 minutes   cook: 20 minutes

1   (14-ounce) prebaked Italian pizza
      bread shell
1   (8-ounce) package shredded Italian
      cheese blend, divided
8   bacon slices, cooked and crumbled
4   plum tomatoes, sliced
½   teaspoon freshly ground pepper

2   large eggs
½   cup milk
¼   cup chopped fresh basil or
      1 teaspoon dried basil

1 Preheat the oven to 425°. Place bread shell on a baking sheet. Sprinkle half of cheese over bread shell; top with bacon, tomatoes, and pepper.

2 Whisk together eggs, milk, and basil; pour in center of pizza (it will spread to edges). Sprinkle with remaining cheese.

3 Bake at 425° for 20 minutes or until set.

Breakfast for Supper

Try this quick, fun treat for breakfast or supper—it's good in a crunch anytime of day. Substitute chopped baked ham or cooked crumbled sausage for the bacon, or leave it out altogether.

So-Easy Pinto Beans 'n' Ham

10 servings

prep: 10 minutes   cook: 9 hours

1   pound dried pinto beans

5½ cups water
1   large onion, chopped
¼   pound cooked ham, chopped
1   clove garlic, minced
1   tablespoon chili powder
1   teaspoon salt
1   teaspoon pepper
¼   teaspoon dried oregano
¼   teaspoon ground cumin

1 Sort and wash beans; place in a 5-quart slow cooker.

2 Stir in 5½ cups water and remaining ingredients.

3 Cook, covered, on HIGH setting 1 hour; reduce heat to LOW setting, and cook 8 more hours, stirring twice.

Slow Cooking—Fast!
The slow cooker will be your new best friend! With a few minutes of prep time in the morning, dinner will be ready and waiting in the evening. Now, how easy is that?! And be sure to use an oven mitt when handling the lid—it's very hot!

Red Beans and Rice

(pictured on facing page)

6 to 8 servings

prep: 5 minutes   cook: 37 minutes

2   tablespoons olive oil
1   (16-ounce) package spicy hickory-
       smoked sausage, cut into ¼" slices
1   large onion, chopped
4   (15-ounce) cans New Orleans-style
       red kidney beans, undrained
2   teaspoons garlic powder, divided
2   teaspoons Cajun seasoning

2   (3.5-ounce) bags boil-in-bag brown
       rice
½   cup butter, softened
Sliced green onions (optional)

1 Heat oil in a Dutch oven over medium-high heat. Add sausage and onion; cook 7 minutes, stirring often. Using a fork, mash 1 can beans in a small bowl. Add mashed beans and remaining 3 cans beans to sausage mixture. Stir in 1 teaspoon garlic powder and the Cajun seasoning. Bring to a boil; reduce heat, and simmer, uncovered, 28 to 30 minutes.

2 Meanwhile, cook rice according to package directions; drain. Add remaining 1 teaspoon garlic powder and the butter, stirring until butter melts. Stir rice mixture into bean mixture. Sprinkle with sliced green onions, if desired. Serve warm.

"If you want to punch up the intensity of the red beans and rice, add a dash or two of your favorite hot sauce just before you dig in.**"**

Crunchy Tuna Salad,
page 76

Chicken Parmesan for Two,
page 91

Cheesy Beef and Bean Tacos

(pictured on facing page)

4 to 6 servings

prep: 7 minutes   cook: 22 minutes

1   pound ground chuck
1   small onion, chopped

1   (1¼-ounce) package taco seasoning
        mix
¾   cup water
1   (15-ounce) can pinto beans, rinsed
        and drained
1   (8-ounce) can tomato sauce
½   cup salsa

1½   cups (6 ounces) shredded sharp
        Cheddar cheese
1   tablespoon chopped fresh cilantro
8   taco shells or 8 (6") flour tortillas
Toppings: shredded lettuce, diced
        tomatoes, sour cream

1 Cook beef and onion in a large non-stick skillet over medium-high heat, stirring until the beef crumbles and is no longer pink; drain.

2 Stir in taco seasoning and water. Cook over medium-high heat 5 to 7 minutes, stirring occasionally. Stir in beans, tomato sauce, and salsa. Mash pinto beans in skillet with fork, leaving some beans whole. Bring to a boil; reduce heat, and simmer, uncovered, 8 to 10 minutes or until liquid thickens.

3 Top evenly with cheese and cilantro. Cover, turn off heat, and let stand 5 minutes or until cheese melts. Serve in taco shells or tortillas and with desired toppings.

Tortilla Tip

To heat flour or corn tortillas, place up to 4 between 2 damp paper towels, and microwave at HIGH for 20 seconds or until thoroughly heated.

Quick Mexican Dinner

5 servings

prep: 7 minutes   cook: 12 minutes

1   pound ground beef

1   (15-ounce) can Spanish rice
1   (15-ounce) can Ranch-style beans,
       undrained
10   (10") flour tortillas
Toppings: shredded cheese, shredded
       lettuce, chopped tomatoes, sour
       cream, sliced jalapeño peppers

1 Cook beef in a large skillet over medium heat, stirring until it crumbles and is no longer pink; drain.

2 Add rice and beans, and cook until thoroughly heated. Spoon evenly onto half of each tortilla; fold tortillas over filling. Serve with desired toppings.

"Here's a quick stovetop solution that's ready to serve in less than 20 minutes—it's cooking the whole family will appreciate."

Curried Beef Stir-fry

6 servings

prep: 15 minutes   cook: 10 minutes

1   pound boneless top sirloin steak
      (see tip on page 22)

2   teaspoons olive oil
1   onion, chopped
2   cloves garlic, minced
3   cups cooked brown rice
1 ½ teaspoons grated fresh ginger or a
      pinch of ground ginger
1 ½ teaspoons curry powder
½   teaspoon salt
½   teaspoon ground red pepper
2   medium apples, coarsely chopped
½   cup apple juice
2   tablespoons slivered almonds,
      toasted (optional)

1 Slice steak diagonally across the grain into wafer-thin slices.

2 Heat oil in a large nonstick skillet over medium-high heat; add steak, onion, and garlic, and sauté 5 to 7 minutes or until onion is tender. Stir in cooked rice and next 6 ingredients; cook until thoroughly heated, stirring often. Sprinkle with almonds, if desired.

"This beefy stir-fry is both hearty and healthy! Check out the apples, almonds, and brown rice that are included in this mouthwatering meal!"

Tex-Mex Casserole

6 servings

prep: 5 minutes   cook: 15 minutes

1   pound ground chuck
¾   cup chopped onion
½   cup chopped celery

1   (16-ounce) can kidney beans,
        drained
1   (11-ounce) can whole kernel corn,
        drained
1   (8-ounce) can tomato sauce
½   cup sliced ripe olives
2   teaspoons chili powder
¾   teaspoon seasoned salt
½   teaspoon pepper

1   cup (4 ounces) shredded sharp
        Cheddar cheese
1   cup crushed corn chips

Additional sliced ripe black olives

1 Combine beef, onion, and celery in a 2½-quart microwave-safe casserole. Cover with wax paper. Microwave at HIGH 5 to 7 minutes or until the beef is no longer pink, stirring at 2-minute intervals to crumble meat; drain.

2 Stir in beans and next 6 ingredients. Cover and microwave at HIGH 5 to 7 minutes or until thoroughly heated, giving dish a half-turn after 3 minutes.

3 Sprinkle with cheese and corn chips. Microwave, uncovered, at MEDIUM-HIGH (70% power) 1 minute or until cheese melts. Sprinkle with additional sliced ripe black olives.

Microwave Magic
No skillet needed here. With the help of your microwave, this savory casserole is on your table in 20 minutes flat!

Sweet Skillet Sirloin

4 servings

prep: 15 minutes   chill: 30 minutes   cook: 10 minutes

3   green onions, minced
2   tablespoons lite soy sauce
1   tablespoon honey
1   teaspoon dark sesame oil
½   teaspoon crushed red pepper
3   teaspoons minced garlic, divided
1   pound beef sirloin, thinly sliced
       (see tip on page 22)

1   teaspoon vegetable oil
Warm cooked brown rice
Cooked frozen mixed vegetables

1 Combine first 5 ingredients and 2 teaspoons minced garlic in a large resealable plastic freezer bag; add beef. Seal and shake to coat. Marinate in the refrigerator 30 minutes.

2 Heat oil in a large skillet over medium-high heat. Add remaining 1 teaspoon minced garlic, and sauté until tender. Add beef mixture; cook 3 to 5 minutes or to desired degree of doneness, stirring often. (Do not overcook, or beef will burn.) Serve with rice and vegetables.

Game Plan

While the beef mixture marinates, begin preparing the brown rice and mixed vegetables. To keep it quick, try the boil-in-bag brown rice. Then 5 minutes is all it takes to cook up this delicious entrée.

Taco Ring

6 to 8 servings

prep: 10 minutes   cook: 37 minutes

1	pound ground round
1	onion, chopped
1	(1¼-ounce) package taco seasoning mix
1	cup (4 ounces) shredded sharp Cheddar cheese
2	(8-ounce) cans refrigerated crescent rolls

Toppings: shredded lettuce, salsa, sour cream

"Tacos turn fancy schmancy encased in flaky crescent rolls."

1 Preheat the oven to 350°. Cook beef and onion in a large skillet over medium-high heat, stirring until the beef crumbles and is no longer pink; drain.

2 Stir in taco seasoning; add water according to package directions. Cook over medium-high heat 3 minutes or until liquid is absorbed. Add cheese, stirring until cheese melts. Remove from heat; set aside.

3 Unroll crescent rolls. Place wide end of triangles on a lightly greased 12" pizza pan, overlapping dough as necessary. Spoon meat mixture in center of dough. Bring smaller ends of triangles over meat, tucking ends under.

4 Bake at 350° for 20 minutes or until rolls are golden. Serve warm with desired toppings.

Stir-fry Pork and Cashews

4 servings

prep: 5 minutes   cook: 6 minutes

1   pound boneless pork loin, cut into
        ½" pieces
⅓   cup stir-fry sauce
2   tablespoons frozen orange juice
        concentrate, thawed
1   tablespoon cornstarch

¼   cup vegetable oil
1   cup dry-roasted or unsalted
        cashews
Warm cooked rice
Orange slices (optional)

1 Stir together first 4 ingredients.

2 Heat oil in a large nonstick skillet over medium-high heat; add pork mixture, and stir-fry 4 to 6 minutes. Stir in cashews. Serve immediately over rice with orange slices, if desired.

"Orange juice concentrate doesn't turn solid when it freezes, so you can spoon it out of the container a tablespoon or two at a time and refreeze the rest. It's one of my quick seasoning secrets!"

Ham 'n' Broccoli Pot Pie

6 servings

prep: 8 minutes   cook: 19 minutes

1   (10-ounce) package frozen chopped
     broccoli, thawed

1   (11-ounce) can sweet whole kernel
     corn, drained
1   (10¾-ounce) can cream of
     mushroom soup, undiluted
2   cups chopped cooked ham
1   (8-ounce) package shredded colby-
     Jack cheese blend
1   (8-ounce) container sour cream
½   teaspoon dry mustard
½   teaspoon pepper

½   (15-ounce) package refrigerated pie
     crusts

1 Preheat the oven to 425°. Arrange
broccoli in a lightly greased oven-
and microwave-safe 10" pie plate or
1½–quart round baking dish.

2 Stir together corn and next 6 ingredients; spoon over broccoli. Cover
loosely with plastic wrap. Microwave at
HIGH 3 to 4 minutes or until heated.

3 Meanwhile, unroll pie crust, and roll
into a 12" circle. Place over warm
ham mixture. Fold edges under, and
crimp; cut slits in top for steam to
escape.

4 Bake at 425° for 15 minutes or until
golden.

Pie Pleaser

Try this version of pot pie as a change from the familiar
chicken pot pie. This one's loaded with ham, corn,
broccoli, and plenty of cheese. For a head start, look
for packaged chopped ham in the meat department
of the supermarket.

Sausage, Peppers, and More

5 servings

prep: 10 minutes   cook: 30 minutes

1	(1¼-pound) package Italian sausage links
1	cup dry white wine
1	medium onion, sliced
1	clove garlic, minced
2	medium-sized green bell peppers, cut into strips
1	(8-ounce) package sliced fresh mushrooms
2	(8-ounce) cans tomato sauce

1 Cook sausage in a 10" cast-iron or heavy skillet; add wine. Bring to a boil; cover, reduce heat, and simmer 10 minutes or until sausage is done. Uncover, bring to a boil, and reduce wine by two-thirds. Remove sausage, reserving drippings in skillet; set sausage aside, and keep warm.

2 Add onion, garlic, bell peppers, and mushrooms to skillet; sauté until tender. Return sausage to skillet; add tomato sauce. Simmer 10 minutes or to desired consistency.

"This chunky blend doubles as a one-dish meal served as is or as a hearty sandwich filling when spooned over sub rolls."

Tortellini Carbonara

2 servings

prep: 5 minutes   cook: 12 minutes

1   (9-ounce) package refrigerated
     cheese-filled tortellini

4   bacon slices
1   clove garlic

⅓   cup shredded Parmesan cheese
¼   cup whipping cream
1   tablespoon minced fresh parsley or
     1 teaspoon dried parsley
¼   teaspoon freshly ground pepper

1 Cook tortellini in a Dutch oven according to package directions; drain tortellini, and set aside.

2 Cook bacon in same pan until crisp; remove bacon, and drain on paper towels, reserving 1½ tablespoons drippings in pan. Crumble bacon, and set aside. Cook garlic in reserved bacon drippings 30 seconds.

3 Return tortellini to pan. Add reserved bacon, Parmesan cheese, and remaining 3 ingredients to tortellini; toss gently. Serve immediately.

❝Cleaning up is a breeze with a one-dish wonder like this pasta dish—you only have to wash one pan!❞

Herb 'n' Veggie Chicken

4 servings

prep: 10 minutes   cook: 21 minutes

¼   cup fine, dry breadcrumbs
       (prepared)
6   tablespoons shredded Parmesan
       cheese, divided
4   skinned and boned chicken breasts

2   tablespoons olive oil

10   large mushrooms, quartered
1   large green bell pepper, thinly sliced
3   large tomatoes, coarsely chopped
1   large clove garlic, pressed
½   teaspoon salt
1   tablespoon dried basil
1   teaspoon dried oregano
Warm cooked rice

1 Combine breadcrumbs and 4 tablespoons Parmesan cheese; dredge
chicken in mixture.

2 Heat oil in a large nonstick skillet
over medium-high heat; add chicken,
and cook 4 minutes on each side or until
golden. Remove chicken from skillet.

3 Add mushrooms and bell pepper to
skillet; sauté 3 minutes. Add tomatoes, garlic, and salt; return chicken to
skillet. Cover, reduce heat, and simmer
10 minutes. Stir in basil, oregano, and
remaining 2 tablespoons Parmesan
cheese. Serve immediately over rice.

Substitution Savvy

Linguine makes a handy substitute for rice. And
if you have the time and access, use ¼ cup
chopped fresh basil and 1 tablespoon chopped
fresh oregano instead of the dried herbs.

Chicken 'n' Vegetable Stir-fry

4 servings

prep: 15 minutes   cook: 15 minutes

2   tablespoons vegetable oil
1   pound chicken breast strips

2   tablespoons water
1   (16-ounce) package frozen broccoli
      stir-fry mix (see tip)
1   red onion, cut into strips
2   red bell peppers, cut into strips
1   (11.75-ounce) bottle stir-fry sauce
Warm cooked rice

1 Heat oil in a large deep skillet over medium-high heat. Add chicken, and stir-fry 2 minutes or until light golden.

2 Add water and vegetables, stirring gently. Cover and cook 8 minutes or until vegetables are crisp-tender, stirring once. Add sauce, and stir-fry 2 minutes. Serve over rice.

Versatile Veggies

If you can't find a 16-ounce package of broccoli stir-fry mix, don't worry. Just pick your favorite from the variety of 16-ounce veggie stir-fry blends in the frozen section of the supermarket.

Turkey à la King

4 to 6 servings

prep: 15 minutes   cook: 16 minutes

1   tablespoon butter
1   bunch green onions, chopped

1   (10¾-ounce) can cream of celery
        soup, undiluted
1   (10¾-ounce) can cream of chicken
        soup, undiluted
1   cup milk
½   teaspoon chicken bouillon granules
¼   teaspoon seasoned pepper
⅛   teaspoon ground white pepper
3   cups chopped cooked turkey
        (see tip)

Split biscuits or toast points

1 Melt butter in a medium saucepan over medium heat; add green onions, and sauté 8 minutes or until tender.

2 Whisk in cream of celery soup and next 5 ingredients until smooth; cook 5 minutes. Stir in turkey; cook 2 to 3 minutes or until thoroughly heated.

3 Serve over split biscuits or toast points.

Here's another solution to leftover holiday turkey—à la king style! Of course, feel free to use chicken when the turkey runs out.

Turkey Tetrazzini

2 servings

prep: 15 minutes   cook: 15 minutes

1½ cups diced deli turkey breast (about
       ½ pound)
½   cup chopped onion
Nonstick cooking spray

¼   cup water
1   (10¾-ounce) can cream of
       mushroom soup, undiluted
¾   cup (3 ounces) shredded sharp
       Cheddar cheese
2   cups warm cooked spaghetti (about
       ¼ pound uncooked)
2   tablespoons chopped fresh parsley
       or 2 teaspoons dried parsley
⅛   teaspoon black pepper
1   (2-ounce) jar diced pimientos,
       drained

1 Heat a large nonstick skillet or
saucepan coated with nonstick cooking spray over medium-high heat. Add
turkey and onion; sauté 3 minutes or
until onion is tender.

2 Stir in water, soup, and cheese;
reduce heat to low, and cook 4 minutes or until cheese melts, stirring until
mixture is smooth. Stir in pasta and
remaining ingredients; cook until thoroughly heated.

Quick Change
Deli-sliced ham works nicely in this casserole instead of
turkey, if you'd prefer.

Microwave Fish 'n' Veggies

4 servings

prep: 10 minutes   cook: 15 minutes

4	(6-ounce) orange roughy fillets
½	teaspoon salt
¼	teaspoon black pepper
½	cup buttermilk dressing
2	cups broccoli florets
1	medium-sized red bell pepper, seeded and cut into strips
1	small onion, cut into strips

1 Place fish in a microwave-safe 7" x 11" baking dish; sprinkle with salt and black pepper. Spread 2 tablespoons dressing over top of each fillet. Arrange broccoli, bell pepper strips, and onion evenly over fish.

2 Cover with heavy-duty plastic wrap; fold back a small corner to allow steam to escape. Microwave at HIGH 13 to 15 minutes or until fish flakes easily with a fork, giving dish a half-turn after 7 minutes.

"You can have a healthy meal ready and on your table in 15 minutes, thanks to the microwave. And cleanup's a cinch since only one dish is used. Now this is my kind of meal!"

New England Clam Chowder

4 to 5 servings

prep: 15 minutes   cook: 25 minutes

4   (6½-ounce) cans minced clams
3   medium-sized potatoes (about
      2 pounds)

6   tablespoons butter, divided
1   small onion, diced

3   cups milk
½   teaspoon salt
¼   teaspoon pepper

1 Drain clams, reserving clam juice. Peel potatoes, and cut into ½" cubes.

2 Melt 2 tablespoons butter over medium heat in a Dutch oven; add diced onion, and sauté until tender. Add reserved clam juice and the potatoes; bring to a boil over medium-high heat. Reduce heat, and simmer 10 minutes or until potatoes are tender, stirring occasionally.

3 Remove 1 cup potatoes with a slotted spoon; mash potatoes and return to Dutch oven. Stir in clams, remaining 4 tablespoons butter, the milk, salt, and pepper; cook until thoroughly heated, stirring occasionally.

Chowder Chatter

There are two main types of chowder—New England style and Manhattan style. The difference? New England style is milk- or cream-based, and Manhattan style is tomato-based. Both are generally made with fish, shellfish, and vegetables—usually potatoes. And both are delicious and hearty enough to make into a meal with some crusty bread and a salad.

Creamy 'Tater 'n' Onion Soup

3 to 4 servings

prep: 15 minutes   cook: 20 minutes

2   tablespoons butter
2   tablespoons all-purpose flour

1   large onion, finely chopped
1   clove garlic, pressed
4   cups chicken broth
2   (14½-ounce) cans whole new
       potatoes, drained and cubed
1   cup milk
1   bunch green onions, sliced
⅛   teaspoon salt
¼   teaspoon pepper

1 Melt butter in a Dutch oven over low heat; whisk in flour until smooth. Cook, whisking constantly, 1 minute.

2 Whisk in chopped onion and garlic, and cook 1 minute. Gradually whisk in chicken broth until blended. Add cubed potatoes and remaining ingredients. Bring mixture to a boil; cover, reduce heat, and simmer 10 minutes or until soup is thoroughly heated, stirring often.

66For a thicker soup, mash about half of the mixture with a potato masher while still in the Dutch oven.99

Sausage-Shrimp Gumbo Soup

6 servings

prep: 6 minutes   cook: 14 minutes

1   (16-ounce) package smoked
      sausage, cut into ½" slices
1   clove garlic, minced
1   (16-ounce) package frozen
      vegetable gumbo mix
1   (14½-ounce) can stewed tomatoes,
      undrained
2   cups chicken broth
2   teaspoons Creole seasoning
¼   teaspoon salt

1   pound peeled, medium-sized fresh
      shrimp (see note)
1   tablespoon filé powder (optional;
      see tip)
Warm cooked rice

1 Cook sausage in a Dutch oven over medium-high heat, stirring constantly, 2 minutes or until browned. Add garlic; cook, stirring constantly, 1 minute. Add vegetable gumbo mix and next 4 ingredients; bring to a boil. Reduce heat, and simmer, uncovered, 5 minutes.

2 Add shrimp; cook 3 minutes or just until shrimp turn pink. Remove from heat; stir in filé powder, if desired. Serve over rice.

Note: Start with 1⅓ pounds of shrimp, if you buy them in the shell.

Filé Facts

Gumbo is usually thickened with okra or filé powder—the latter is made from young ground sassafras leaves and is regarded as quintessential to gumbo and other Creole dishes. Filé is added after the gumbo has finished cooking because it will become stringy if allowed to boil. It can also be passed around the table so each person can thicken their gumbo to their own preference. Use filé sparingly—a small amount can thicken a whole pot of gumbo! Look for filé powder in the spice section or with gourmet foods in your supermarket.

Meatball Stew

4 to 5 servings

prep: 10 minutes   cook: 20 minutes

2   potatoes, cut into ½" cubes
1   small onion, chopped
1   (10-ounce) package frozen mixed
        vegetables
2   (15-ounce) cans tomato sauce
1   (10½-ounce) can beef broth,
        undiluted
1¼ cups water
½   teaspoon dried Italian seasoning
¼   teaspoon pepper

3   dozen frozen cooked meatballs

1 Bring all ingredients except meatballs to a boil in a large saucepan. Cover, reduce heat, and simmer 10 minutes.

2 Stir in meatballs; cover and simmer 5 to 10 minutes or until vegetables are tender and meatballs are thoroughly heated.

❝Make quick work of this stew by using commercially prepared meatballs. It'll be so welcome at the end of a long, busy day.❞

Very Veggie Chili

8 to 10 servings

prep: 15 minutes   cook: 30 minutes

2   tablespoons vegetable oil
1   large sweet onion, diced
1   large green bell pepper, diced
2   cloves garlic, minced

1   (12-ounce) package burger-style
        vegetable crumbles
1   large zucchini, diced
1   (11-ounce) can whole kernel corn,
        undrained
2   (15-ounce) cans pinto beans, rinsed
        and drained
2   (15-ounce) cans tomato sauce
2   (10-ounce) cans diced tomato and
        green chilies, undrained
1   (1¾-ounce) package Texas-style
        chili seasoning mix

1 Heat oil in a large stockpot over medium-high heat. Add onion, bell pepper, and garlic; sauté 5 minutes or until tender.

2 Stir in vegetable crumbles and remaining ingredients. Bring to a boil; reduce heat, and simmer, uncovered, 20 minutes, stirring often.

"This veggie chili is so hearty you won't miss the meat! But if you've got meat-lovin' folks in your family, go ahead and brown a pound of ground chuck and use it instead of the vegetable crumbles."

No-Cook Meals

"No-cook meals? You betcha! Pick any of these tasty sandwiches and salads for a meal that's hassle-free.**"**

Open-Faced Avocado Sandwiches

4 servings

prep: 12 minutes

1	avocado, peeled and cut into thin slices
¼	cup Italian dressing
1	tablespoon mayonnaise
4	oatmeal or whole wheat bread slices, toasted
4	(1-ounce) process American cheese slices
8	thin tomato slices
1	cup coarsely shredded iceberg lettuce (see tip)

1 Toss avocado slices gently with Italian dressing; drain avocado well, reserving dressing.

2 Spread mayonnaise evenly over 1 side of each bread slice. Top bread slices with avocado, cheese slices, tomato slices, and lettuce.

3 Drizzle sandwiches evenly with reserved Italian dressing, and serve immediately.

Lessons on Lettuce
For crisp iceberg lettuce, discard the outer leaves, and rinse and core the lettuce as soon as you get home from the supermarket. Whirl it in a salad spinner and chill it, wrapped in paper towels in a resealable plastic bag, until ready to use—at least an hour or up to 5 days.

Mediterranean Pitas

4 servings

prep: 15 minutes

4   (6") pita bread rounds
1   (3-ounce) package cream cheese,
        softened

2   cups coarsely chopped fresh baby
        spinach
1   (4-ounce) package crumbled feta
        cheese
1   cup chopped tomato
1   (16-ounce) can garbanzo beans
        (chickpeas), rinsed and drained
1   (2.25-ounce) can sliced ripe black
        olives
¼   cup chopped fresh basil
¼   cup Greek dressing

1 Cut 1½" off the top of each pita round to form a pocket. Spread cream cheese evenly inside each pita pocket.

2 Combine spinach and next 5 ingredients. Pour dressing over spinach mixture, tossing to coat. Fill each pita pocket with spinach mixture.

66No passport required to savor the flavors of the Mediterranean. You'll find them stuffed inside the pockets of these great-tasting sandwiches!99

Mozzarella-Pepper Bagel Sandwiches

4 servings

prep: 8 minutes   chill: 2 hours

2	tablespoons olive oil
2	tablespoons red wine vinegar
1	to 2 cloves garlic, pressed
1	teaspoon dried basil
¼	teaspoon freshly ground pepper
4	bagels, split
8	(1-ounce) mozzarella cheese slices
½	(12-ounce) jar roasted red bell peppers, drained
4	small onion slices
4	tomato slices

1 Combine first 5 ingredients in a jar; cover tightly, and shake vigorously. Drizzle over cut sides of bagels; top each bagel bottom with 1 slice of cheese.

2 Cut peppers into strips; place evenly over cheese-topped bagel bottoms with onion, tomatoes, and remaining cheese. Replace bagel tops, and seal in plastic wrap. Chill at least 2 hours before serving.

“Who says sandwiches have to be piled with meat to fill you up? Try this veggie sandwich with mozzarella, roasted bell peppers, tomatoes, and onions atop a bagel—perfect for a quick lunch or dinner.”

Curried Tuna-Apple Sandwiches

3 servings

prep: 10 minutes

¼ cup mayonnaise
1 tablespoon lemon juice
½ teaspoon curry powder
⅛ teaspoon garlic powder
1 (6-ounce) can albacore tuna, drained
1 small Granny Smith apple, chopped
1 celery rib, chopped
¼ cup raisins
2 tablespoons diced onion
6 whole grain bread slices

1 Stir together first 4 ingredients. Stir in tuna and next 4 ingredients. Spread mixture on whole grain bread.

Can-Do Tuna

Albacore is the mildest tuna and is the only type that can be called "white." It's also worth the added expense, so don't substitute since chunks of tuna are the main attraction in this sandwich.

Mango-Chicken Pita Sandwiches

8 servings

prep: 10 minutes

1 (10-ounce) package shredded angel hair cabbage slaw
1 Granny Smith apple, diced
½ cup plain yogurt
1 teaspoon grated lemon rind
½ teaspoon dry mustard
4 pita bread rounds, halved
1 (6-ounce) package refrigerated cooked chicken strips
1 cup mango chutney (see tip)

1 Combine first 5 ingredients. Layer pita halves evenly with chicken, mango chutney, and slaw mixture.

Look for mango chutney in the condiment section of your supermarket. Any leftover chutney can be served with chicken or fish entrées or over a block of cream cheese as an appetizer.

Very Gouda Chicken Sandwiches

4 servings

prep: 18 minutes

1	(2½-pound) roasted whole chicken
¼	cup honey mustard
¼	cup mayonnaise

4	(6½") submarine rolls
1	(5-ounce) Gouda cheese round, cut into 12 thin slices
12	thin tomato slices

Leaf lettuce

1 Slice chicken from bone; set chicken aside. Stir together mustard and mayonnaise.

2 Split rolls horizontally; spread with mustard mixture. Top each roll bottom with desired amount of chicken slices and 3 cheese slices. (Reserve any extra chicken for another use.) Top each with 3 tomato slices and the lettuce. Top with roll tops. Serve immediately.

"No need to mess with slicing the Gouda yourself! Buy your cheese from the deli counter at the supermarket and have it thinly sliced."

Dilly Beef Sandwiches

6 servings

prep: 10 minutes   stand: 30 minutes

¾   cup sour cream
2   tablespoons dry onion soup mix
1   teaspoon prepared mustard
1   teaspoon prepared horseradish

12   rye bread slices
1   pound thinly sliced roast beef
Salt (optional)
6   green leaf lettuce leaves
12   (¼"-thick) tomato slices
18   dill pickle slices

1 Stir together first 4 ingredients; let stand 30 minutes.

2 Top 6 bread slices with roast beef; sprinkle with salt, if desired. Spread sour cream mixture evenly over roast beef. Top evenly with lettuce, tomato slices, and dill pickles. Cover with remaining bread slices. Cut sandwiches in half diagonally, and serve immediately.

Hot 'n' Spicy
If you like to spice things up a bit, look for peppercorn-studded deli roast beef for this handful of a sandwich.

Roast Beef Subs

4 servings

prep: 12 minutes

1 ¼ cups fresh corn kernels or frozen
     whole kernel corn, thawed
⅓   cup diced red bell pepper
¼   cup diced red onion
¼   cup Caesar dressing

4   (6½") submarine rolls
4   red leaf lettuce leaves
8   (¼"-thick) tomato slices
8   (1-ounce) slices lean cooked roast
     beef

1 Combine first 4 ingredients, and set aside.

2 Cut a ¼"-thick slice off top of each roll; set tops aside. Hollow out centers of rolls, leaving ½"-thick shells. (Reserve inside of rolls for another use.) Place 1 lettuce leaf in bottom portion of each roll. Spoon corn mixture evenly over lettuce; top each serving with 2 tomato slices and 2 slices roast beef. Cover with roll tops.

66This sub is good anytime of year, but the flavor is at its best during the summer when corn and tomatoes are at their peak.99

Ham 'n' Pineapple Slaw Sandwiches

4 servings

prep: 10 minutes

3 cups shredded cabbage
2 cups chopped cooked ham
1 (8-ounce) can pineapple tidbits, undrained
1 cup (4 ounces) shredded Cheddar cheese
2/3 cup mayonnaise
1/2 teaspoon salt
1/2 teaspoon pepper
4 (6½") submarine rolls

1 Combine all ingredients except rolls, stirring gently. Spoon mixture onto bottoms of rolls; cover with tops, and serve immediately.

These cool salad sandwiches are just what you want in your hand for lunch during those long, hot days of summer.

Bean 'n' Bacon Wraps

4 servings

prep: 20 minutes

½   (8-ounce) package cream cheese,
    softened
1   tablespoon taco sauce
4   (6") flour tortillas
1   cup canned black beans, rinsed and
    drained
½   small green bell pepper, diced
¼   cup real bacon pieces
¼   cup (1 ounce) shredded Cheddar
    cheese

1 Stir together cream cheese and taco sauce; spread mixture evenly on 1 side of each tortilla. Top with black beans and remaining ingredients.

2 Roll up tortillas tightly. Wrap in plastic wrap; refrigerate until chilled.

Sandwich Slump?
Break out of the ordinary the next time you're making sandwiches, and use one of these different breads:

- whole wheat buns
- French bread loaves
- flour tortillas
- submarine rolls

- pita bread rounds
- steak rolls
- kaiser rolls

Black Bean Salad

6 servings

prep: 13 minutes   chill: 30 minutes

1   (15-ounce) can black beans, rinsed
     and drained
1½   cups frozen whole kernel corn,
     thawed
½   cup chopped green bell pepper
⅓   cup chopped fresh cilantro
⅔   cup tequila-lime marinade (see tip)
½   teaspoon ground cumin

Romaine lettuce leaves
2   large avocados, sliced
½   cup (2 ounces) shredded Monterey
     Jack cheese

1 Combine first 4 ingredients. Stir in marinade and cumin. Cover and chill 30 minutes.

2 Spoon bean mixture over lettuce; arrange avocado slices around salad, and sprinkle with cheese.

Flavor Find
Look for tequila-lime marinade in the marinade and sauce section of large supermarkets.

Chef's Salad

6 servings

prep: 10 minutes

8 cups mixed salad greens
2 cups chopped mixed fresh
    vegetables (see tip)
1 small red onion, cut in half and
    sliced
3 cups coarsely chopped cooked
    chicken
1 large avocado, peeled and sliced
¼ cup real bacon bits
3 cups croutons
1 (16-ounce) bottle Ranch-style
    dressing

1 Toss together first 3 ingredients. Top with chicken and avocado; sprinkle with bacon and croutons. Serve with dressing.

Make a Rainbow!
Chopped mixed fresh vegetables add a rainbow of color to this hearty salad. A combination of yellow squash, cucumber, broccoli, red bell pepper, and carrot showers it with lots of flavors.

Cucumber-Crab Salad

4 servings

prep: 12 minutes

½ cup sugar
½ cup white wine vinegar
1 teaspoon soy sauce
½ teaspoon salt
½ teaspoon pepper
2 cucumbers, thinly sliced
2 celery ribs, thinly sliced
1 small onion, thinly sliced
1 cup fresh lump crabmeat, drained
    (see tip)
4 tomatoes, sliced

1 Whisk together first 5 ingredients in a medium bowl. Add cucumbers and next 3 ingredients, and toss well. Serve over tomato slices.

Canned Crab

A 6-ounce can of drained crabmeat can be substituted for the fresh. To make the canned taste fresher, soak it in ice water for 10 minutes, drain, and pat dry.

Make-Ahead Shrimp Salad

4 to 6 servings

prep: 12 minutes   chill: 2 hours

1	cup mayonnaise
½	cup finely chopped celery
¼	cup finely chopped onion
¼	cup ketchup
2	teaspoons prepared mustard
2	teaspoons lemon juice
1	teaspoon Worcestershire sauce
½	teaspoon garlic powder
¼	teaspoon salt
1	pound frozen peeled and deveined salad shrimp, thawed
1	cup grape tomatoes, halved
7	cups shredded lettuce (1 head iceberg)

1 Combine first 9 ingredients in a large bowl; stir in shrimp and tomatoes. Cover and chill 2 hours or until ready to serve. Serve over lettuce.

"Get a jump start with this easy make-ahead dish—you can make it in the morning and let it chill until you're ready to serve it for lunch or dinner."

Crunchy Tuna Salad

(pictured on page 38)

6 servings

prep: 7 minutes   chill: 1 hour

1	(12-ounce) can white tuna in water, drained
1	cup frozen petite green peas, thawed
¾	cup chopped celery
¾	cup mayonnaise
1	tablespoon lemon juice
1	teaspoon curry powder
½	teaspoon salt
¼	teaspoon pepper
1	(10-ounce) package mixed salad greens
¾	cup chow mein noodles

1 Combine first 8 ingredients in a large bowl. Cover and chill at least 1 hour.

2 Serve over greens, and sprinkle with chow mein noodles.

"This is a great salad to serve with Melba toast or plain or garlic-flavored bagel chips. It's also good served between 2 slices of multigrain bread. It's a winner any way you choose!"

Confetti Chicken Salad

4 to 6 servings

prep: 15 minutes   chill: 15 minutes

3   tablespoons lemon juice, divided
¼   cup plain yogurt
⅓   cup mayonnaise
1   teaspoon salt
2   teaspoons hot sauce
¼   teaspoon ground cumin
4   cups chopped cooked chicken
      breasts
½   cup thin carrot strips
¼   cup finely chopped red bell pepper
4   green onions, finely chopped
1   tablespoon chopped fresh cilantro

2   avocados
Red leaf lettuce leaves

1 Stir together 2 tablespoons lemon juice, the yogurt, and next 4 ingredients in a medium bowl until blended. Stir in chicken and next 4 ingredients. Cover and chill at least 15 minutes or up to 1 hour.

2 Peel and thinly slice avocados; toss avocado slices in remaining 1 tablespoon lemon juice. Spoon salad over lettuce leaves, and arrange avocado slices around chicken salad.

"If you're in a big hurry, you can substitute ½ cup store-bought dressing, such as restaurant-style creamy lime-cilantro dressing, for the first 6 ingredients of this recipe."

Greek Chicken Salad

7 servings

prep: 20 minutes

1 head romaine lettuce, torn into small pieces
2 tomatoes, cut into ¾" pieces
1 large cucumber
½ cup chopped fresh parsley
½ cup chopped green onions
1 teaspoon dried mint leaves
3 (6-ounce) packages grilled chicken strips (about 3 cups)
½ cup crumbled feta cheese
¼ cup kalamata or ripe black olives, pitted and coarsely chopped
1 (8-ounce) bottle Greek salad dressing
3 (6") pita rounds, halved

1 Combine first 6 ingredients in a large bowl, tossing gently; top with chicken, feta cheese, and olives. Drizzle with Greek salad dressing, and serve with pita halves.

66 Enjoy this alongside a soup or sandwich, or stuff it into a pita half, and drizzle with dressing. 99

Vegetable Patch Chicken Salad

4 servings

prep: 15 minutes   chill: 30 minutes

3	cups chopped cooked chicken
½	cup frozen petite green peas, thawed
½	cup prepared cucumber Ranch-style dressing
¼	cup seeded, chopped cucumber
2	tablespoons minced onion
2	tablespoons minced red bell pepper
2	tablespoons minced fresh parsley or 2 teaspoons dried parsley
1	tablespoon lemon juice

1 Stir together all ingredients in a large bowl. Cover and chill at least 30 minutes before serving.

Preparing this salad is like a skip through the vegetable patch since it's chockful of 'em.

Roast Beefy Salad

4 servings

prep: 15 minutes

2 onion slices, cut ¼" thick
3 green onions, cut into 3" pieces
18 fresh mint leaves
1 large jalapeño pepper, seeded
   (see tip)
3 fresh cilantro sprigs
¾ cup lime juice
2 tablespoons fish sauce (see note)

1 pound thinly sliced Italian-seasoned
   deli roast beef, cut into strips
Boston lettuce leaves
¼ cup chopped cocktail peanuts
4 green onions, diagonally sliced

1 Process first 7 ingredients in a food processor until blended.

2 Arrange beef strips over lettuce, and sprinkle with peanuts and sliced green onions. Serve with dressing.

Note: If you can't find fish sauce in the Asian section of your supermarket, substitute 1 tablespoon soy sauce and 1 tablespoon water.

Hot Tip
When seeding jalapeños, it's best to wear rubber gloves. The seeds and veins in the pepper are hot and can burn your hands—and your eyes, too.

Easy Entrées

"Yes sirree, with entrées as easy as these, you'll have dinner for the gang in no time!"

Quick Shrimp Chowder

6 to 8 servings

prep: 15 minutes   cook: 20 minutes

2   tablespoons butter
1   medium onion, chopped
2   (10¾-ounce) cans cream of potato
      soup, undiluted
3½ cups milk
¼   teaspoon ground red pepper
1½ pounds medium-sized peeled, fresh
      shrimp (see tip)
1   cup (4 ounces) shredded Monterey
      Jack cheese
Oyster crackers (optional)

1 Melt butter in a Dutch oven over medium heat; add onion, and sauté 8 minutes or until tender. Stir in soup, milk, and pepper; bring to a boil. Add shrimp; reduce heat, and simmer 5 minutes or just until shrimp turn pink, stirring often. Stir in cheese until melted. Serve immediately. Serve with oyster crackers, if desired.

Substitution Savvy

You can substitute 1½ pounds thawed frozen peeled shrimp, 1½ pounds peeled crawfish tails, or 3 cups chopped cooked chicken for the 1½ pounds medium-sized fresh shrimp. If you want to start with unpeeled shrimp, buy 2 pounds in the shell.

Black, White, and Red All Over Soup

3 servings

prep: 5 minutes   cook: 25 minutes

1   (15½-ounce) can white hominy,
       rinsed and drained
1   (15-ounce) can black beans, rinsed
       and drained
1   (14½-ounce) can chili-style diced
       tomatoes, undrained
1   (14-ounce) can chicken broth
1   teaspoon chopped fresh cilantro
½   teaspoon chili powder
½   teaspoon ground cumin

1 Combine all ingredients in a large saucepan; cook over medium heat until soup is thoroughly heated, stirring occasionally.

66*What's black, white, and red all over? This super-duper easy soup. No high-tech appliance needed here—just a good can opener!*99

Crunchy Catfish Fingers

8 servings

prep: 20 minutes   cook: 22 minutes

8   (4-ounce) catfish fillets
¾   teaspoon seasoned salt, divided

1½   cups milk
2   tablespoons Dijon mustard
2   cups crushed crispy corn cereal
         squares (about 5 cups uncrushed)
¼   cup cornstarch
½   teaspoon pepper

Nonstick cooking spray

1 Preheat the oven to 375°. Cut each fillet lengthwise into 3 strips. Sprinkle evenly with ½ teaspoon seasoned salt.

2 Whisk together milk and mustard in a shallow dish. In another shallow dish, combine crushed cereal, cornstarch, pepper, and remaining ¼ teaspoon seasoned salt. Dip fish in milk mixture; dredge in cereal mixture. Arrange fish fingers on a lightly greased wire rack.

3 Place rack in an aluminum foil-lined broiler pan. Lightly coat fish with nonstick cooking spray. Bake at 375° for 20 to 22 minutes or until fish flakes easily with a fork.

“Shhh! Crushed cereal is my secret ingredient for these extra crunchy catfish fingers.”

Grilled Salmon with Dipping Sauce

6 servings

prep: 5 minutes   cook: 26 minutes

2   cups soy sauce
2   tablespoons canola oil
8   pieces crystallized ginger or
        ⅛ teaspoon ground ginger
2   cloves garlic, minced
2   cups sugar
6   (4-ounce) salmon fillets

2   (12-ounce) packages broccoli slaw
4   green onions, chopped
1   tablespoon sesame seeds, toasted
Salt and pepper to taste

1 Spray cold grill rack with nonstick cooking spray; preheat the grill to medium-high heat (350° to 400°). Combine soy sauce, oil, ginger, and garlic in a small saucepan over medium heat. Stir in sugar. Cook 10 minutes or until sugar dissolves, stirring occasionally. Remove from heat. (Mixture will thicken.) Reserve 1½ cups soy sauce mixture, and set aside. Brush both sides of salmon evenly with remaining soy sauce mixture; cover and let stand 10 minutes.

2 Place salmon on grill rack; grill, covered, 4 to 6 minutes on each side or until fish flakes easily with a fork.

3 Toss together broccoli slaw, green onions, sesame seeds, and ½ cup of reserved soy sauce mixture; top with grilled salmon. Season with salt and pepper to taste. Serve with remaining 1 cup reserved soy sauce mixture for dipping.

Double Dip

The dipping sauce will keep in the refrigerator, covered, for several weeks. Warm sauce over medium-low heat on cooktop before serving. You can use it as a marinade for steak or shrimp, too.

Creole Shrimp with Garlic Cream Sauce

2 to 3 servings

prep: 10 minutes   cook: 8 minutes

1   pound large unpeeled, fresh shrimp
¾   teaspoon Creole seasoning
⅛   teaspoon ground red pepper

1   tablespoon olive oil
2   cloves garlic, minced
2   green onions, chopped
1   cup whipping cream
2   tablespoons chopped fresh parsley
          or 2 teaspoons dried parsley
3   tablespoons lemon juice
Warm cooked angel hair pasta or
          spaghetti

1 Peel shrimp, and devein, if desired. Combine Creole seasoning and red pepper; sprinkle over shrimp, tossing to coat.

2 Heat olive oil in a large skillet over medium-high heat; add shrimp. Cook shrimp 3 minutes, stirring often. Add garlic and green onions; cook 1 minute, stirring often. Add whipping cream; cook 2 minutes, stirring often. Stir in parsley and lemon juice. Serve immediately over pasta.

Some Like It Hot!

You can change the heat of this dish to suit your tastes by increasing the amount of ground red pepper or by adding hot sauce. Remember that Creole seasoning contains red pepper as well.

Garlic Shrimp and Grits

4 servings

prep: 5 minutes   cook: 16 minutes

3 cups water
1 cup whipping cream
¼ cup butter
1 teaspoon salt
1 cup quick-cooking grits, uncooked

1 pound medium-sized peeled,
      cooked fresh shrimp (see tip)
1 cup (4 ounces) extra-sharp
      shredded Cheddar cheese
2 cloves garlic, minced

1 Bring first 4 ingredients to a boil in a large saucepan over medium-high heat. Reduce heat to medium; whisk in grits. Cook, whisking constantly, 7 to 8 minutes or until smooth.

2 Stir in shrimp, cheese, and garlic. Cook 1 to 2 minutes or until thoroughly heated.

Do It Yourself

If you want to peel and cook the shrimp yourself, start with 2 pounds medium-sized unpeeled, fresh shrimp.

Shrimp and Sausage Jambalaya

6 to 8 servings

prep: 13 minutes   cook: 32 minutes

1   (16-ounce) package smoked
        sausage, sliced
1   cup chopped green bell pepper
1   cup chopped onion
2   (10-ounce) cans mild diced
        tomatoes and green chilies,
        undrained
2   cups chicken broth
1   cup water
2   teaspoons Cajun seasoning
1   teaspoon garlic powder

2   cups uncooked long-grain rice
1   pound uncooked peeled and
        deveined shrimp (see tip)

1 Cook sausage in a Dutch oven over medium heat 5 minutes or until browned. Add bell pepper and onion; cook over medium-high heat 3 minutes or until vegetables are almost tender. Add tomatoes and next 4 ingredients; bring to a boil.

2 Add rice; reduce heat, cover, and simmer 15 minutes. Add shrimp; cover and cook 4 minutes or until shrimp turn pink and rice is tender.

If time's not an issue, and you'd rather peel and devein the shrimp yourself, you'll need to start with 1⅓ pounds of fresh shrimp in the shell.

Glazed Roasted Chicken Thighs

4 servings

prep: 10 minutes   chill: 8 hours   cook: 30 minutes

½ cup teriyaki sauce

¼ cup frozen orange juice concentrate,
  thawed and undiluted

3 tablespoons dark sesame oil

4 cloves garlic, minced

1 teaspoon salt

½ teaspoon ground pepper

8 chicken thighs

1 Stir together all ingredients except chicken; cover and reserve half of mixture in the refrigerator.

2 Trim excess fat from chicken; rinse and pat dry. Place in a large resealable plastic freezer bag, and pour remaining teriyaki mixture over chicken; seal bag, and marinate in refrigerator 8 hours, turning occasionally.

3 Preheat the oven to 450°. Remove chicken from marinade, discarding marinade. Place chicken, skin side up, on an aluminum foil-lined 10" x 15" rimmed baking sheet.

4 Bake at 450° for 30 minutes or until a meat thermometer inserted in chicken thigh registers 180° and meat is tender, basting once. Skim fat from pan juices; stir remaining juices into reserved teriyaki mixture. Brush chicken with teriyaki mixture.

"*Let these chicken thighs marinate while you're at work, and then pop them in the oven to bake when you get home. Dinner is served! Cleanup's a breeze, too, when you line the baking sheet with aluminum foil!*"

Barbecue-Battered Chicken Fingers

6 to 8 servings

prep: 7 minutes   cook: 7 minutes per batch

3   pounds skinned and boned chicken
    breasts

3   cups all-purpose flour
1½   teaspoons seasoned salt
1½   teaspoons pepper
¾   teaspoon garlic powder

2   cups buttermilk
¾   cup honey smoke barbecue sauce
2   large eggs

Vegetable oil
Honey smoke barbecue sauce

1 Cut each chicken breast into 3" strips; set aside.

2 Combine flour and next 3 ingredients in a large shallow dish.

3 Whisk together buttermilk, ¾ cup barbecue sauce, and the eggs in a bowl. Dredge chicken pieces in flour mixture; dip in buttermilk mixture, and dredge again in flour mixture. (If flour gets gummy, just press into chicken pieces.)

4 Pour oil to a depth of 1½" in a deep skillet or Dutch oven; heat to 360°. Fry chicken, in batches, 5 to 7 minutes or until golden. Drain on wire racks over paper towels. Serve with additional barbecue sauce.

Barbecue-Battered Pork Chops

For a delicious alternative to chicken fingers, use this recipe with pork chops. Just substitute 3 pounds boneless breakfast pork chops for chicken, and proceed as directed. Serve cooked chops in biscuits, if desired.

Chicken Parmesan for Two

(pictured on page 39)

2 servings

prep: 20 minutes   cook: 16 minutes

1   cup Italian-seasoned breadcrumbs
2   tablespoons all-purpose flour
½   teaspoon ground red pepper

2   skinned and boned chicken breasts
2   egg whites, lightly beaten

1   tablespoon olive oil

1½ cups prepared pasta sauce
1   cup (4 ounces) shredded mozzarella
     cheese
¼   cup grated Parmesan cheese

1 Preheat the oven to 400°. Combine breadcrumbs, flour, and red pepper in a small bowl; set aside.

2 Place chicken between 2 sheets of heavy-duty plastic wrap, and flatten to ¼" thickness, using a meat mallet or rolling pin. Dip each chicken breast in egg whites, and coat with breadcrumb mixture. Dip again in egg mixture, and coat again in breadcrumb mixture.

3 Heat oil in a large skillet over medium heat; add chicken, and cook 3 minutes on each side or until done.

4 Place chicken breasts in a single layer in a lightly greased 8" square baking dish. Top evenly with pasta sauce and cheeses. Bake at 400° for 10 minutes or until cheeses melt.

❝In a little over 30 minutes, you can have a romantic dinner for two. Add a salad and Italian bread, and wait for sparks to fly!❞

Honey-Pecan Chicken Breasts

4 servings

prep: 15 minutes   cook: 22 minutes

2   tablespoons soy sauce
2   tablespoons honey
¾   cup crushed cornflakes cereal
3   tablespoons finely chopped pecans

4   skinned and boned chicken breasts
½   teaspoon salt
½   teaspoon pepper

1 Preheat the oven to 425°. Combine soy sauce and honey in a shallow bowl; set aside. Combine cornflakes and pecans in another shallow bowl; set aside.

2 Sprinkle chicken evenly with salt and pepper. Dip chicken breasts in soy sauce mixture; dredge in cornflake mixture, pressing mixture onto chicken, if necessary. Place chicken breasts on a lightly greased foil-lined baking sheet.

3 Bake at 425° for 20 to 22 minutes or until chicken is golden and cooked through.

❝Cereal and pecans make up the crunchy topping for these chicken breasts that are dipped in a honey-soy sauce mixture. Easy, quick, and delicious—my kind of recipe!❞

Limeade Chicken

8 servings

prep: 10 minutes   cook: 25 minutes

8   skinned and boned chicken breasts
¼   teaspoon salt
⅛   teaspoon pepper
Nonstick cooking spray

1   (6-ounce) can frozen limeade
      concentrate, thawed and undiluted
3   tablespoons brown sugar
3   tablespoons ketchup

1 Sprinkle chicken with salt and pepper. Heat a nonstick skillet coated with nonstick cooking spray over medium-high heat. Add chicken, and cook 4 minutes on each side; remove from skillet.

2 Add limeade concentrate, brown sugar, and ketchup to skillet; bring to a boil. Cook, stirring constantly, 5 minutes or until thickened. Return chicken to skillet; cover and cook 10 minutes or until done.

The secret to these tasty chicken breasts is a can of frozen limeade concentrate—it shortens my prep time and heightens the flavor!

Oven-Fried Chicken

8 servings

prep: 10 minutes   cook: 20 minutes

1¼ cups Italian-seasoned
     breadcrumbs
¼ cup grated Parmesan cheese

½ cup mayonnaise
½ teaspoon salt
½ teaspoon poultry seasoning
¼ teaspoon ground red pepper
8 skinned and boned chicken breasts

1 Preheat the oven to 425°. Stir together breadcrumbs and Parmesan cheese in a shallow dish.

2 Stir together mayonnaise and next 3 ingredients in another dish. Brush both sides of chicken with mayonnaise mixture, and dredge in breadcrumb mixture. Place in a lightly greased aluminum foil-lined 10" x 15" rimmed baking sheet.

3 Bake at 425° for 20 minutes or until done.

“When it comes to fast meals from scratch, it's hard to beat chicken breasts. With this recipe, they emerge from the oven nice 'n' golden in just 20 minutes!”

Chicken Scaloppine

4 servings

prep: 5 minutes   cook: 8 minutes

½   cup all-purpose flour
1   teaspoon salt
¾   teaspoon seasoned pepper
1 ½   pounds chicken cutlets

2   tablespoons olive oil

1   cup white wine or chicken broth

1 Combine first 3 ingredients in a shallow dish; dredge chicken cutlets in flour mixture.

2 Heat oil in a large skillet over medium-high heat; add chicken, and cook 1 to 2 minutes on each side or until done. Remove from skillet, and keep warm.

3 Add wine to skillet; cook 1 to 2 minutes or until liquid is reduced by half, stirring to loosen particles from bottom of skillet.

4 Arrange cutlets on a serving platter, and drizzle with sauce.

Sautéing Secrets

The secret to sautéing thinly sliced cutlets is to have both the pan and oil hot enough to sear the meat—you should hear the food hiss as soon as it hits the pan.

Chicken and Dumplings

6 servings

prep: 15 minutes   cook: 15 minutes

Nonstick cooking spray
3   celery ribs, sliced
2   carrots, sliced
6   cups chicken broth
½   teaspoon poultry seasoning
½   teaspoon pepper

1⅔ cups biscuit baking mix
⅔   cup milk

3   cups chopped cooked chicken

1 Heat a large Dutch oven coated with nonstick cooking spray over medium-high heat. Add celery and carrots, and sauté 6 minutes or until tender. Stir in broth, poultry seasoning, and pepper; bring to a boil.

2 Meanwhile, stir together biscuit mix and milk until blended. Turn dough out onto a heavily floured surface; roll or pat dough to ⅛" thickness. Cut into 2" x 3" strips.

3 Drop strips, 1 at a time, into boiling broth; stir in chicken. Cover, reduce heat, and simmer 8 minutes, stirring occasionally.

Dumplings Gone Light

You can lighten up this Southern classic without sacrificing taste. Substitute 3 (14-ounce) cans of low-sodium fat-free chicken broth, reduced-fat biscuit baking mix, and fat-free milk for their regular counterparts.

Asian Chicken Noodle Bowl

4 to 6 servings

prep: 12 minutes   cook: 10 minutes

6 ounces rice noodles or vermicelli
noodles

8 cups hot water

2 tablespoons dark sesame oil
3 cloves garlic, minced
2 cups matchstick carrots
¾ cup chopped green onions (about
1 bunch)
2 cups shredded cooked chicken
5 cups finely chopped napa cabbage
(about 1 small head)

½ cup sesame ginger marinade
½ cup chicken broth
½ teaspoon crushed red pepper

1 Soak noodles in 8 cups hot water for
10 minutes; drain and set aside.

2 Meanwhile, heat oil in a large skillet
over medium-high heat; add garlic
and carrots, and sauté 3 minutes or until
tender. Add green onions, chicken, and
cabbage; cook, stirring constantly, 3
minutes.

3 Combine marinade and broth; stir
into cabbage mixture. Bring to a boil;
boil 1 minute. Remove from heat; stir
in red pepper. Serve warm over noodles.

*"Check out all the new varieties of
marinades that're now available at your
local supermarket. They're loaded with
flavor and save lots of time!"*

Flank Steak with Tomato-Olive Relish

(pictured on page 3)

6 servings

prep: 15 minutes   cook: 29 minutes

1½   pounds flank steak
¾   teaspoon salt
¾   teaspoon coarsely ground pepper
3   tablespoons olive oil

2   cloves garlic, thinly sliced
½   cup red wine or chicken broth
1   (14½-ounce) can Italian-style diced
        tomatoes
½   cup pitted oil-cured black olives,
        chopped
1   tablespoon balsamic vinegar
3   tablespoons minced fresh parsley or
        1 tablespoon dried parsley

1 Sprinkle flank steak evenly with salt and pepper. Heat oil in a large skillet over medium-high heat. Add steak, and cook 8 to 9 minutes on each side or to desired degree of doneness.

2 Drain, reserving 1 tablespoon drippings in skillet; add garlic, and sauté 1 minute. Add wine, tomatoes, olives, and vinegar; cook 10 minutes or until reduced by half. Stir in parsley.

3 Cut steak diagonally across grain into thin slices, and serve with tomato relish.

This relish goes great with flank steak, but I think you'll agree that it'll complement chicken or pork just as well.

Steak Parmesan

4 servings

prep: 5 minutes   cook: 26 minutes

½   cup fine, dry breadcrumbs
      (prepared)
½   cup grated Parmesan cheese,
      divided
1   large egg, lightly beaten
1   tablespoon water
⅛   teaspoon pepper
4   cubed sirloin steaks (about 1 pound)

¼   cup vegetable oil
1   cup prepared pizza sauce

1 Preheat the oven to 325°. Combine breadcrumbs and ¼ cup cheese in a shallow dish. Combine egg, water, and pepper in another shallow dish. Dip steaks in egg mixture; dredge in breadcrumb mixture.

2 Heat oil in a skillet over medium heat. Add steaks, and cook 3 minutes on each side. Arrange steaks in an 8" square baking dish. Top with pizza sauce; bake at 325° for 20 minutes. Sprinkle with remaining ¼ cup cheese.

❝My *Speedy Garlic Mashed Potatoes on page 147 would be oh-so-delicious with this hearty entrée. See for yourself, or look for other quick sides that begin on page 135.*❞

Sensational Beef Pie

4 servings

prep: 5 minutes   cook: 26 minutes

1   (25-ounce) package frozen beef and
        vegetable combination
¼   cup water
¼   teaspoon pepper

½   (15-ounce) package refrigerated pie
        crusts

1 Preheat the oven to 425°. Place beef and vegetables in a 9" oven- and microwave-safe pie plate; add ¼ cup water. Cover loosely with plastic wrap, and microwave at HIGH 6 minutes, stirring after 3 minutes. Sprinkle mixture evenly with pepper.

2 Unroll pie crust, and place on top of beef mixture; fold edges under, and crimp. Cut 4 slits in center of crust.

3 Bake at 425° for 18 to 20 minutes or until golden.

Sensational Substitutes

Try a package of frozen chicken or roasted turkey and vegetable combination for the beef, if desired.

Open-Faced Meatball Sandwiches

6 servings

prep: 10 minutes   cook: 35 minutes

1   tablespoon olive oil
1   small sweet onion, diced
1   small green bell pepper, diced
1   clove garlic, pressed

1   (26-ounce) jar five-cheese spaghetti
    sauce
1   tablespoon chopped fresh basil or
    1 teaspoon dried basil
1   (32-ounce) package frozen cooked
    Italian-style meatballs

6   slices garlic-butter Texas toast
1   cup shredded Parmesan cheese
2   cups (8 ounces) shredded
    mozzarella cheese
Toppings: shredded lettuce, chopped
    tomatoes, chopped bell peppers,
    sliced ripe black olives

1 Heat oil in a large skillet over medium-high heat; add onion, bell pepper, and garlic, and sauté 3 minutes.

2 Stir in sauce, basil, and frozen meatballs; cook 25 minutes or until thoroughly heated, stirring often.

3 Prepare Texas toast according to package directions. Spoon meatball mixture evenly over toast; top evenly with cheeses and desired toppings.

❝Get your knife and fork out for this hearty sandwich. This meatball mixture is spooned over Texas toast and piled high with two types of cheese, lettuce, tomatoes, bell peppers, and black olives!❞

Beef and Bean Chimichangas

(pictured on cover)

10 servings

prep: 18 minutes   cook: 35 minutes

1   pound ground chuck
¾   cup chopped onion
¾   cup diced green bell pepper
1   (1¼-ounce) package taco seasoning
        mix
⅔   cup water
1   (11-ounce) can whole kernel corn,
        drained
1   (8-ounce) bottle taco sauce

1   (16-ounce) can refried beans
10   (8") flour tortillas
1   (8-ounce) package shredded
        Monterey Jack cheese with
        peppers
Butter-flavored nonstick cooking spray

Toppings: shredded lettuce, diced
        tomatoes, sour cream

1 Preheat the oven to 425°. Combine first 3 ingredients in a large skillet over medium-high heat; cook, stirring until the beef crumbles and is no longer pink. Drain. Stir in taco seasoning mix and water; cook 5 minutes over medium heat. Add corn and taco sauce; cook 1 to 2 minutes or until heated. Remove from heat, and set aside.

2 Spread a thin layer of beans evenly onto each of the tortillas. Spoon ½ cup beef mixture down the center of each tortilla, and top with shredded cheese. Fold sides in and roll up, burrito-style; place seam side down on a lightly greased rimmed baking sheet. Spray tortillas with nonstick cooking spray.

3 Bake, uncovered, at 425° for 22 minutes or until golden. Serve with desired toppings.

66*These Mexican favorites are baked instead of fried. Same great taste and a lot less mess! You might say we did a 'changa' to the 'chimis.'*99

Lasagna Casserole

6 to 8 servings

prep: 15 minutes   cook: 35 minutes

8   ounces uncooked rotini pasta

1   pound ground chuck
½   teaspoon salt
1   (15-ounce) can tomato sauce
1   (10-ounce) can diced tomatoes and
     green chilies with garlic, oregano,
     and basil

1   (8-ounce) package cream cheese,
     softened
1   cup ricotta cheese
4   cups (16 ounces) shredded
     mozzarella cheese, divided
¼   cup chopped fresh parsley or
     1 tablespoon dried parsley

1 Preheat the oven to 350°. Cook pasta according to package directions; drain and place in a greased 9" x 13" baking dish. Cover and set aside.

2 While pasta cooks, cook beef and salt in a large skillet over medium-high heat, stirring until beef crumbles and is no longer pink; drain. Meanwhile, stir together tomato sauce and diced tomatoes and chilies.

3 Stir together cream cheese, ricotta cheese, 2 cups mozzarella cheese, and the parsley; spoon beef mixture and cheese mixture over pasta, spreading to reach edges of dish. Pour tomato mixture over cheese mixture. Sprinkle with remaining 2 cups mozzarella cheese. Bake, uncovered, at 350° for 30 minutes or until bubbly. Let stand 10 minutes before cutting.

Quick Change

One pound of Italian pork sausage makes a fine substitute for ground chuck when you're ready for a change of taste.

Creamy Dijon Lamb Chops

(pictured on facing page)

4 servings

prep: 4 minutes   cook: 20 minutes

8	(2"-thick) lamb loin chops, trimmed
½	teaspoon salt
¼	teaspoon freshly ground pepper
1	tablespoon olive oil
2	cloves garlic, minced
¾	cup whipping cream
2	tablespoons Dijon mustard
¼	teaspoon dried thyme

1 Sprinkle lamb chops with salt and pepper. Heat oil in a heavy skillet over medium heat. Add chops, and cook 7 minutes on each side or until a meat thermometer inserted in thickest part registers 150° (medium-rare). Place chops in a serving dish, reserving 1 tablespoon drippings in skillet.

2 Sauté garlic in reserved drippings over medium heat 30 seconds. Stir in cream, mustard, and thyme. Bring to a boil over medium heat; cook 3 minutes, stirring constantly. Serve sauce over chops.

Game Plan for Dinner
- Cook the mashed potatoes in microwave (see page 147).
- Begin cooking lamb chops in skillet.
- While potatoes and chops cook, steam some fresh or frozen green beans.
- When menu is complete, stir up the creamy Dijon sauce so it will be hot when served with the lamb chops.

Creamy Dijon Lamb Chops, steamed green beans, and Speedy Garlic Mashed Potatoes, page 147

Greek Pita Pizzas,
page 124

Grilled Asian Pork Chops,
page 111

Spicy Pork Tenderloin

(pictured on facing page)

6 servings

prep: 10 minutes   cook: 22 minutes

2   (1-pound) pork tenderloins
1   tablespoon olive oil
1½ tablespoons Caribbean jerk
     seasoning

1 Brush tenderloins with olive oil, and rub evenly with seasoning.

2 Preheat the grill to medium-high heat (350° to 400°). Place pork on grill rack; grill, covered, 10 to 12 minutes on each side or until a meat thermometer inserted in thickest part registers 155°. Remove from grill, and let stand, covered, 10 minutes or until temperature reaches 160°. Slice thinly, and serve.

From Everyday—to Gourmet!

If you're in search of an easy entrée that can go from everyday to gourmet, this is it. Caribbean seasoning adds a touch of sweet heat to these grilled tenderloins. Pick up a jar of peach or mango salsa to serve with them.

Greek-Style Baked Pork Chops

4 servings

prep: 10 minutes   cook: 11 minutes

½ cup chopped roasted red bell
    peppers
1 tablespoon chopped fresh parsley or
    1 teaspoon dried parsley
1 tablespoon lemon juice
5 cloves garlic, pressed
½ teaspoon dried oregano
¼ cup all-purpose flour
½ teaspoon salt
1 teaspoon freshly ground black
    pepper
4 (½"-thick) boneless loin pork chops
    (about 6 ounces)

1 tablespoon butter

½ cup crumbled feta cheese
⅓ cup pitted kalamata or ripe black
    olives, chopped

1 Preheat the oven to 400°. Combine first 5 ingredients in a small bowl, and set aside. Combine flour, salt, and black pepper in a large resealable plastic freezer bag. Add pork chops; seal and shake to coat.

2 Melt butter in a 9" cast-iron skillet over medium-high heat (see tip). Add chops; cook 2 minutes on each side or until browned. Spoon reserved bell pepper mixture evenly over chops.

3 Bake in skillet, covered, at 400° for 5 minutes or until done. Sprinkle with cheese and olives.

Quick Tip
If you don't have a cast-iron skillet, wrap the handle of a large nonstick skillet with heavy-duty aluminum foil. This should make your regular skillet safe for a quick stint in the oven.

Grilled Asian Pork Chops

(pictured on page 107)

6 servings

prep: 7 minutes   chill: 10 minutes   cook: 8 minutes

6   tablespoons soy sauce
1   teaspoon pepper
2   teaspoons toasted sesame oil
2   teaspoons lime juice
6   cloves garlic, minced
6   (¼"- to ½"-thick) boneless pork chops

1 Preheat the grill to medium-high heat (350° to 400°). Combine all ingredients except pork chops in a large shallow dish or large resealable plastic freezer bag; add pork chops. Cover or seal, and marinate in the refrigerator 10 minutes. Remove chops from marinade, discarding marinade.

2 Place chops on grill rack; grill, covered, 3 to 4 minutes on each side or until done.

These boneless chops need to marinate only 10 minutes—just enough time for the grill to preheat.

Saucy Ham Steak

4 servings

prep: 8 minutes   cook: 10 minutes

¼   cup prepared mustard
¼   cup ginger ale
2   tablespoons dark brown sugar
½   teaspoon prepared horseradish
1   (1"-thick) slice fully cooked ham,
        (about 2 pounds)

1 Combine first 4 ingredients in a small bowl, and stir well. Spread about half of mustard mixture over ham.

2 Spray cold grill rack with nonstick cooking spray; preheat the grill to medium-high heat (350° to 400°). Place ham on grill rack; grill, covered, 4 to 5 minutes on each side, basting occasionally with remaining mustard mixture.

So Saucy

This feisty mustard mixture is a good basting sauce for chicken or turkey, too.

Pizza and Pasta

....

"Not only do pizza and pasta rank as top family favorites, they're also the perfect solution to dinner on the double!"

Cheesesteak Pizza

4 servings

prep: 7 minutes   cook: 15 minutes

1   (14-ounce) package prebaked Italian
     pizza bread shell
¼   cup olive oil, divided
2   cloves garlic, crushed

1   small onion, sliced
1   small green bell pepper, sliced
1   (8-ounce) package sliced fresh
     mushrooms
1   teaspoon Worcestershire sauce
8   ounces shaved deli roast beef

1½ cups (6 ounces) shredded Italian-
     style five-cheese blend, divided

1 Preheat the oven to 450°. Place bread shell on a rimless baking sheet. Combine 3 tablespoons olive oil and the garlic in a small bowl; brush over bread shell, and set aside.

2 Heat remaining 1 tablespoon oil in a large skillet over medium-high heat. Add onion, pepper, and mushrooms; sauté 5 minutes or until vegetables are tender. Stir in Worcestershire sauce and roast beef.

3 Sprinkle ½ cup cheese over bread shell. Spoon roast beef mixture over cheese; top with remaining 1 cup cheese.

4 Bake at 450° for 10 minutes or until cheese melts. Cut into wedges.

Crispy, Crusty Perfection

To bake any of these pizzas with a crispy crust, bake pizza directly on the center rack of your oven. Use a baking sheet with no side edges like a giant spatula to easily transfer the pizza directly to the oven rack. Use the same baking sheet to remove the pizza from the oven.

Meaty Pizza Pie

4 to 5 servings

prep: 10 minutes   cook: 30 minutes

1   (15-ounce) package refrigerated pie
     crusts
2   cups spaghetti sauce with meat
16 pepperoni slices

1   cup (4 ounces) shredded mozzarella
     cheese

1 Preheat the oven to 425°. Unroll pie crusts; stack pie crusts, and press together. Place pie crust on a parchment paper-lined baking sheet. Spread meat sauce over crust, leaving a 1" border; top with pepperoni slices. Fold crust edges slightly over filling.

2 Bake on lower rack of oven at 425° for 15 minutes. Sprinkle with cheese, and bake 15 more minutes or until bubbly and golden. Cool 5 minutes. Cut into wedges.

66Use your family's favorite leftover meat sauce for this hearty weeknight meal. A green salad makes a great go-along.**99**

Reuben Pizza

4 servings

prep: 10 minutes   cook: 10 minutes

1   (14-ounce) package prebaked Italian
        pizza bread shell
½   cup Thousand Island dressing
12   ounces thinly sliced corned beef
1½   cups sauerkraut, drained
1½   to 2 cups (6 to 8 ounces) shredded
        Swiss cheese
1   teaspoon caraway seeds

Chopped dill pickles (optional)

1 Preheat the oven to 450°. Place bread shell on a baking sheet. Spread dressing over bread shell; top with corned beef slices and sauerkraut. Sprinkle with shredded Swiss cheese and caraway seeds.

2 Bake pizza at 450° for 10 minutes or until cheese melts. Top with pickles, if desired, and cut into wedges; serve immediately.

❝This classic deli staple enjoys new life as a family-friendly pizza. Feel free to use deli ham instead of corned beef if you have picky eaters.❞

Santa Fe Pizza

(pictured on page 2)

4 servings

prep: 8 minutes   cook: 17 minutes

1   (14-ounce) package prebaked Italian
       pizza bread shell

½   (16-ounce) roll ground hot pork
       sausage
½   cup finely chopped red bell pepper
1   jalapeño pepper, seeded and diced
       (see tip)

1   cup chunky salsa
1   teaspoon chili powder
½   cup canned black beans, rinsed and
       drained
1   cup (4 ounces) shredded Cheddar
       and Monterey Jack cheese

2   tablespoons chopped fresh cilantro
Sour cream (optional)

1 Preheat the oven to 450°. Place bread shell on a baking sheet. Bake at 450° for 8 minutes; set aside.

2 Meanwhile, cook sausage in a large skillet over medium-high heat, stirring until it crumbles and is no longer pink. Drain sausage, and return to skillet. Add peppers; cook 3 minutes or until tender.

3 Combine salsa and chili powder; spread over crust. Top with sausage mixture and black beans; sprinkle with cheese.

4 Bake at 450° for 6 minutes or until cheese melts. Sprinkle with cilantro. Cut into wedges. Serve with sour cream, if desired.

"Remember to wear rubber gloves when seeding jalapeño peppers so you don't burn your hands—or eyes—if you accidentally touch them. The seeds and veins are also hot."

German-Style Pizza

4 servings

prep: 8 minutes   cook: 15 minutes

½ cup spicy brown mustard
1   (14-ounce) package prebaked Italian
    pizza bread shell
1   (10-ounce) can chopped sauerkraut,
    drained and squeezed dry
8   ounces fully cooked smoked
    bratwurst, chopped (see tip)
1   teaspoon fennel seeds
1   cup (4 ounces) shredded Swiss
    cheese

1 Preheat the oven to 450°. Spread mustard over bread shell. Top with sauerkraut and remaining ingredients.

2 Transfer pizza directly to center rack of oven using a baking sheet with no sides as a giant spatula. Bake at 450° for 15 minutes or until cheese melts and bread shell is golden. Remove pizza from oven, using rimless baking sheet. Cut into wedges.

Quick Brats

Buying precooked bratwurst quickens the assembly of this pizza. But if you have time to allow for longer cooking, try using fresh bratwurst for authentic German taste.

Chicken Fajita Pizza

4 servings

prep: 10 minutes   cook: 15 minutes

1   clove garlic, halved
1   (14-ounce) package prebaked Italian
      pizza bread shell
½   cup salsa
1½   cups (6 ounces) shredded Monterey
      Jack cheese with peppers, divided
1   cup chopped cooked chicken

1   tablespoon olive oil
1   red onion, thinly sliced
1   green bell pepper, sliced

2   tablespoons chopped fresh cilantro
Salsa

1 Preheat the oven to 450°. Rub cut sides of garlic over bread shell; discard garlic. Spread salsa in a thin layer over bread shell. Top with ½ cup cheese and the chicken; set aside.

2 Heat olive oil in a large skillet over medium-high heat. Add onion and pepper; cook 5 minutes or until tender. Spoon onion mixture over chicken; top with remaining 1 cup cheese.

3 Transfer pizza directly to center rack of oven using a baking sheet with no sides as a giant spatula. Bake at 450° for 10 minutes or until golden and cheese melts. Remove pizza from oven, using rimless baking sheet. Top pizza with cilantro. Cut into wedges. Serve with additional salsa.

“Try this Mexican-American favorite on a pizza. Salsa, onion, bell pepper, and cilantro atop chicken give this pizza real Southwestern sizzle!”

Roasted Vegetable Pizza

4 servings

prep: 7 minutes   cook: 32 minutes

1   (14-ounce) package prebaked Italian pizza bread shell

1   cup zucchini, halved lengthwise and sliced into ½"-thick slices
½   cup thinly sliced red onion
½   cup chopped red bell pepper
½   cup frozen whole kernel corn, thawed
1   tablespoon olive oil
1   tablespoon balsamic vinegar

1   cup prepared tomato-basil pasta sauce
¾   cup (3 ounces) shredded pizza cheese blend

1 Preheat the oven to 450°. Place bread shell on a baking sheet. Bake at 450° for 8 minutes; remove from oven, and set aside.

2 Combine zucchini and next 5 ingredients in a bowl; toss to combine. Spread on a lightly greased 10" x 15" rimmed baking sheet.

3 Bake at 450° for 20 minutes or until vegetables are roasted.

4 Spread pasta sauce over prepared bread shell. Spoon vegetables over sauce; sprinkle with cheese. Bake 4 more minutes or until cheeses melt. Cut into wedges.

❝Roasting brings out the natural sweetness in many vegetables, so you don't want to skip this vital part—it's what makes this pizza ooh so good!❞

Grilled Pizza

4 servings

prep: 15 minutes   cook: 6 minutes

1   (8-ounce) can tomato sauce
3   cloves garlic, minced
1   teaspoon dried basil
1   teaspoon ground oregano
1   teaspoon crushed red pepper

1   (16-ounce) package frozen bread
        dough, thawed
2   tablespoons olive oil, divided

½   cup grated Parmesan or Romano
        cheese
½   cup sliced ripe olives
1   (6-ounce) jar marinated artichoke
        hearts, drained and coarsely
        chopped
1   cup (4 ounces) shredded mozzarella
        cheese

1 Combine first 5 ingredients, and set aside.

2 Roll dough into an 8" circle on a lightly floured surface; brush dough with 1 tablespoon oil.

3 Preheat the grill to medium-high heat (350° to 400°). Place dough, oiled side down, on grill rack; brush top with remaining oil. Grill, uncovered, 2 minutes or until grill marks appear.

4 Spoon tomato sauce mixture over dough; sprinkle with Parmesan cheese and remaining ingredients.

5 Grill, covered, 4 minutes or until pizza crust is slightly crisp. Remove from grill, and cut into wedges.

The grill's not just for burgers anymore! Grilled pizza is the rage these days and mine will have the gang ravin' over its crispy crust and smoky flavor.

Cheesy Mexican Pizza

4 servings

prep: 15 minutes   cook: 10 minutes

1   (14-ounce) package prebaked Italian
     pizza bread shell
1   cup refried beans
½   cup sour cream
¼   cup black bean dip

1   (14½-ounce) can diced tomatoes
2   cups (8 ounces) shredded Cheddar
     cheese
1   cup (4 ounces) shredded Monterey
     Jack cheese with peppers

1 Preheat the oven to 450°. Place bread shell on a baking sheet. Stir together refried beans, sour cream, and bean dip; spread over bread shell.

2 Drain tomatoes, and pat dry with paper towels; spoon over bean mixture. Sprinkle with cheeses.

3 Bake at 450° for 10 minutes or until cheese melts. Cut into wedges.

Lighten Up

This recipe can easily be lightened up by substituting fat-free refried beans, fat-free or light sour cream, and reduced-fat cheeses for their regular counterparts.

Mediterranean Pizza

6 servings

prep: 15 minutes   cook: 10 minutes

1   (16-ounce) can garbanzo beans
        (chickpeas), rinsed and drained
1   (7-ounce) jar roasted red bell
        peppers, drained and chopped
2   cloves garlic
2   tablespoons olive oil
2   tablespoons lemon juice
½   teaspoon salt
¼   teaspoon black pepper

1   (10-ounce) package prebaked Italian
        pizza bread shell
1   (8-ounce) package feta cheese,
        crumbled
3   plum tomatoes, sliced
¼   cup pitted kalamata or ripe black
        olives, chopped
1   teaspoon dried oregano

1 Preheat the oven to 450°. Process first 7 ingredients in a blender or food processor until smooth, stopping to scrape down sides.

2 Spread garbanzo bean mixture over bread shell. Top with feta cheese and remaining ingredients.

3 Transfer pizza directly to center rack of oven using a baking sheet with no sides as a giant spatula. Bake at 450° for 8 to 10 minutes or until golden. Remove pizza from oven, using rimless baking sheet. Cut into wedges.

"You'll be guaranteed lots of 'oohs' and 'aahs' when you serve up this Mediterranean-inspired pizza."

Greek Pita Pizzas

(pictured on page 106)

6 servings

prep: 18 minutes   cook: 12 minutes

1   (12-ounce) package 6" pita bread
     rounds
1   cup tomato-basil pasta sauce
1   small red onion, halved lengthwise
     and cut into thin strips
½   cup pitted kalamata or ripe black
     olives, halved
2   (4-ounce) packages crumbled feta
     cheese

¼   cup fresh basil, chopped

1 Preheat the oven to 450°. Place pita
rounds on a baking sheet. Spread pita
rounds with pasta sauce. Top with red
onion and olives; sprinkle with cheese.

2 Bake at 450° for 10 to 12 minutes or
until cheese melts. Sprinkle with basil
before serving. Cut into wedges.

In the Round

Place pita rounds on a baking sheet with rounded
side down. This keeps the sauce and toppings neatly
on the pita round.

Nutty Pesto Pizza

4 servings

prep: 10 minutes   cook: 10 minutes

½   cup pesto
½   cup pizza sauce
1   (12") refrigerated pizza crust
4   to 6 plum tomatoes, sliced
1   cup (4 ounces) shredded mozzarella
     cheese
1   cup (4 ounces) shredded Havarti
     cheese
1   (4-ounce) package goat cheese,
     crumbled
½   cup (2 ounces) shredded Parmesan
     cheese
2   tablespoons pine nuts

1 Preheat the oven to 425°. Spread pesto and pizza sauce over pizza crust; top with tomatoes and remaining ingredients.

2 Transfer pizza directly to center rack of oven using a baking sheet with no sides as a giant spatula. Bake at 425° for 8 to 10 minutes or until cheese is bubbly. Remove pizza from oven, using rimless baking sheet. Cut into wedges.

Any way you slice it, this pizza is a speedy meal! All you need is 20 minutes—start to finish. If you don't have a pizza wheel handy, use your kitchen scissors to cut slices.

Grilled Portobello Pizzas

8 servings

prep: 13 minutes   cook: 10 minutes

1   cup tomato-basil pasta sauce
1   clove garlic, minced
1   tablespoon Worcestershire sauce
½   cup chopped fresh basil, divided
8   large Portobello mushroom caps
1   (8-ounce) bottle Italian dressing

1   cup (4 ounces) shredded Italian
    cheese blend

1 Stir together first 3 ingredients and ¼ cup basil; set aside. Combine mushroom caps and Italian dressing in a large resealable plastic freezer bag, turning to coat. Let stand 2 to 3 minutes.

2 Remove mushrooms from marinade, discarding marinade. Spray cold grill rack with nonstick cooking spray; preheat the grill to medium-high heat (350° to 400°).

3 Place mushroom caps, gill side up, on heated grill rack, and grill, covered, 3 to 4 minutes on each side. Turn caps, gill side up, and spoon sauce mixture into each.

4 Grill, covered, 2 more minutes or until thoroughly heated. Sprinkle with shredded cheese and remaining ¼ cup chopped basil; serve immediately.

Double Duty

To turn this recipe into burgers, serve Grilled Portobello Pizzas on warm toasted hamburger buns with desired toppings.

Ranch Chicken Pasta Salad

6 servings

prep: 15 minutes   cook: 9 minutes

8	ounces uncooked bow tie pasta
3	cups chopped cooked chicken
1	pint grape tomatoes, halved
½	cup diced red onion
½	cup freshly grated Parmesan cheese
½	cup chopped pecans, toasted
1	teaspoon freshly ground black pepper
1	cup Ranch-style dressing

1 Cook pasta according to package directions; drain. Rinse under cold water, and drain.

2 Combine pasta, chicken, and next 5 ingredients in a large bowl; stir well. Add dressing, and toss to coat. Cover and chill.

Kids and adults alike will enjoy this tasty pasta salad that's tossed with chicken and pecans and coated with Ranch-style dressing.

Cheesy Chicken Penne

4 to 6 servings

prep: 15 minutes   cook: 10 minutes

8   ounces uncooked penne pasta

1   (16-ounce) loaf pasteurized
       prepared cheese product, cubed
1   (8-ounce) container sour cream
½   cup milk
2½ cups chopped cooked chicken

1 Cook pasta according to package directions; drain.

2 Meanwhile, cook cubed cheese, sour cream, and milk over medium-low heat, stirring constantly, 5 minutes or until cheese melts. Stir in pasta and chicken, and cook until thoroughly heated.

Spicy Cheesy Chicken Penne
For a little heat, substitute 2 (8-ounce) loaves pasteurized prepared cheese product with peppers for the regular cheese product, and then prepare recipe as directed.

Creamy Chicken-Artichoke Pasta

4 servings

prep: 17 minutes   cook: 11 minutes

8   ounces uncooked linguine

2   tablespoons butter
4   cloves garlic, pressed
⅓   cup dry white wine
1   (8-ounce) package cream cheese,
        softened
1   cup whipping cream
1   tablespoon Dijon mustard

2   (6-ounce) packages oven-roasted
        diced cooked chicken breast
1   (7½-ounce) jar marinated quartered
        artichoke hearts, drained and
        chopped
½   cup freshly grated Parmesan cheese
Freshly ground black pepper

1 Prepare pasta according to package directions. Drain and keep warm.

2 Meanwhile, melt butter in a large nonstick skillet over medium-high heat. Add garlic; sauté 1 minute. Add wine; cook 1 minute. Add cream cheese, whipping cream, and mustard; cook over medium heat 3 minutes or until melted, stirring constantly.

3 Add chicken, artichokes, and pasta; cook 5 minutes or until thoroughly heated, stirring occasionally. Sprinkle with Parmesan cheese and pepper. Serve immediately.

"You'll want to have your salad and bread ready when you sit down to eat this pasta dish. It's best served immediately, while the sauce is still hot, creamy, and yummy!"

Layered Spaghetti Casserole

6 servings

prep: 5 minutes   cook: 32 minutes

8   ounces uncooked spaghetti

1   pound ground chuck
1   small onion, chopped
1   (26-ounce) jar pasta sauce with
        mushrooms

¼   cup butter
¼   cup all-purpose flour
1   (12-ounce) can evaporated milk
½   cup grated Parmesan cheese
¼   teaspoon salt
¼   teaspoon pepper

2   cups (8 ounces) shredded sharp
        Cheddar cheese, divided

1 Cook pasta according to package directions; drain.

2 Meanwhile, cook beef and onion in a skillet over medium-high heat, stirring until the beef crumbles and is no longer pink; drain. Combine pasta, meat mixture, and pasta sauce in a large bowl; toss to combine. Set aside.

3 Preheat the oven to 400°. Melt butter in a saucepan over medium heat. Stir in flour; cook 1 minute. Gradually whisk in milk; cook 5 minutes or until thickened. Remove from heat; stir in Parmesan cheese, salt, and pepper.

4 Pour half of spaghetti mixture into a lightly greased 7" x 11" baking dish; pour cheese sauce over spaghetti. Sprinkle with 1 cup Cheddar cheese. Top with remaining spaghetti mixture, and sprinkle with remaining 1 cup Cheddar cheese. Bake at 400° for 15 minutes or until cheese melts.

❝I sure don't mind leftovers of this creamy spaghetti—it's just as good or better the next day. Only problem is that you might not have any left!❞

Spicy Beef and Artichoke Linguine

5 servings

prep: 10 minutes   cook: 22 minutes

10	ounces uncooked linguine
½	pound ground round
2	cups vegetable primavera spaghetti sauce
1	cup water
2	tablespoons tomato paste
½	teaspoon crushed red pepper
3	cloves garlic, crushed
1	(14-ounce) can quartered water-packed artichoke hearts, drained

1 Cook pasta according to package directions; drain. Cover, set aside, and keep warm.

2 Meanwhile, cook beef in a large non-stick skillet over medium-high heat, stirring until it crumbles and is no longer pink; drain well, and return beef to skillet.

3 Add spaghetti sauce and next 4 ingredients to pan; stir well. Bring to a boil; reduce heat, and simmer, uncovered, 10 minutes. Stir in artichokes; cover and simmer 2 minutes. Serve meat mixture over pasta.

"Jarred sauce never tasted so good! Here, it's dressed up with ground round, artichoke hearts, garlic, and a punch of crushed red pepper."

Fusilli with Sausage and Peppers

8 servings

prep: 10 minutes   cook: 15 minutes

1   (16-ounce) package fusilli, uncooked

1   pound Italian sausage
1   large onion, chopped
1   red or green bell pepper, cut into
       strips
1½ teaspoons dried basil
1   (14-ounce) can Italian
       herb-seasoned chicken broth

1   cup (4 ounces) shredded Parmesan
       cheese

1 Cook pasta according to package directions; drain.

2 Meanwhile, remove and discard sausage casings. Cook sausage and next 3 ingredients in a skillet over medium-high heat, stirring until the sausage crumbles and is no longer pink. Drain well; return sausage mixture to skillet. Stir in broth; cook 5 minutes or until thoroughly heated, stirring often.

3 Spoon sausage mixture over pasta; sprinkle with cheese, and serve immediately.

Pasta Pointers

Fusilli is a spiral-shaped pasta—similar to a corkscrew. The Italian translation actually means "twists." This pasta also goes well with thick sauces.

Eggplant Fettuccine

4 servings

prep: 15 minutes   cook: 12 minutes

1   (12-ounce) package fettuccine,
      uncooked

1   to 2 tablespoons olive oil
1   medium onion, chopped
3   cloves garlic, minced
1   medium eggplant, peeled and
      cubed
1   large red bell pepper, sliced

2   (14½-ounce) cans pasta-style
      tomatoes
½   cup grated Parmesan cheese

1 Cook fettuccine according to package directions; drain and place in a large serving bowl.

2 Meanwhile, heat oil in a large skillet over medium-high heat. Add onion and next 3 ingredients; cook, stirring constantly, 10 minutes or until vegetables are tender.

3 Stir in tomatoes; spoon mixture over pasta, and sprinkle with cheese.

66This meatless entrée is marvelous! In less than 30 minutes, you can have a mouth-watering dish on your table—and you don't have to be a vegetarian to enjoy it.99

Ravioli with Creamy Pesto Sauce

6 servings

prep: 5 minutes   cook: 15 minutes

1   cup whipping cream
1   (3-ounce) jar capers, drained
1   (2.82-ounce) jar pesto sauce

2   (9-ounce) packages refrigerated
      cheese-filled ravioli, uncooked
2   tablespoons pine nuts, toasted
      (see tip)

1 Combine first 3 ingredients in a medium saucepan. Cook over low heat until thoroughly heated, stirring often (do not boil).

2 Meanwhile, cook pasta according to package directions; drain. Toss pasta with cream mixture, and sprinkle with pine nuts. Serve immediately.

Toasting Tip

Toasting brings out the full flavor of nuts. Just place a small amount in a dry skillet over medium heat for a few minutes, stirring often. Watch them! The smaller the pieces, the quicker they cook.

Speedy Sides

❝Speeding right through
these veggies and side dishes
is a breeze with my list of
convenient ingredients and
no-fuss preparation steps.**❞**

Asparagus Amandine

8 servings

prep: 5 minutes   cook: 15 minutes

2   pounds fresh asparagus

2   tablespoons butter
¼   cup sliced almonds
2   tablespoons diced red bell pepper
1   tablespoon lemon juice
½   teaspoon salt
½   teaspoon black pepper

1 Snap off tough ends of asparagus (see tip). Cook asparagus in boiling salted water to cover in a large skillet 3 minutes or until crisp-tender; drain. Plunge asparagus into ice water to stop the cooking process; drain.

2 Melt butter in a large skillet over medium heat; add almonds, and sauté 2 to 3 minutes or until golden. Add asparagus and red bell pepper; cook 3 to 5 minutes. Toss with lemon juice, salt, and black pepper; serve immediately.

It's a Snap!

The easiest way to snap off tough ends of asparagus is to hold it by the tip end in one hand and bend the other end until it snaps. It'll snap where the most tender part begins.

Green Beans with Grape Tomatoes

8 servings

prep: 12 minutes   cook: 18 minutes

2   quarts water
2   pounds fresh green beans, trimmed

6   tablespoons butter
1   pint grape tomatoes, halved
1   tablespoon chopped fresh thyme or
        1 teaspoon dried thyme
2   teaspoons sugar
1   teaspoon salt
½   teaspoon pepper

1 Bring 2 quarts water to a boil in a Dutch oven; add beans, and cook 8 minutes or until crisp-tender; drain. Plunge into ice water to stop the cooking process; drain.

2 Melt butter in a large skillet over medium heat 6 to 7 minutes or until butter begins to brown. Add green beans, and sauté until tender. Stir in grape tomatoes and remaining ingredients. Serve immediately.

Great Grape Tomatoes

Grape tomatoes are small and oval-shaped with red or yellow skin and have a sweet flavor like summer tomatoes. Look for them at your local supermarket.

Floret Medley

6 to 8 servings

prep: 8 minutes   cook: 18 minutes

5   cups fresh broccoli florets (about
      1 pound)
5   cups fresh cauliflower florets (about
      1 pound)

⅓   cup butter
1   large red bell pepper, chopped
      (about 1 cup)
3   green onions, chopped
2   cloves garlic, pressed
2   tablespoons Dijon mustard
¾   teaspoon salt
½   teaspoon freshly ground black
      pepper

1 Arrange broccoli and cauliflower florets in a steamer basket over boiling water. Cover and steam 8 minutes.

2 Melt butter in a Dutch oven over medium-high heat. Add broccoli mixture, bell pepper, and remaining ingredients; sauté 5 to 7 minutes or until crisp-tender. Serve immediately.

Speedy Substitute

If you're short on time, use 2 (16-ounce) packages fresh broccoli and cauliflower florets to make preparing this side dish super speedy.

Garlicky Cabbage

4 to 5 servings

prep: 5 minutes   cook: 35 minutes

1   small cabbage (about 2 pounds)

3   tablespoons olive oil
6   cloves garlic, finely sliced
½   cup chicken broth
1   teaspoon coarse or kosher salt

Freshly ground pepper to taste

1 Preheat the oven to 350°. Remove outside leaves and stalk from cabbage; cut cabbage into 4 wedges.

2 Heat oil in a skillet over medium-high heat. Sauté garlic 1 to 2 minutes or until golden. Add cabbage to skillet, cut sides down; cook 5 minutes. Turn to other cut sides, and cook 2 to 3 minutes. Stir in broth, and sprinkle evenly with salt. Transfer cabbage mixture to a 7" x 11" baking dish.

3 Bake at 350° for 20 to 25 minutes or until crisp-tender. Sprinkle evenly with pepper. Serve immediately.

Cabbage Choices
Look for green and red cabbage year-round in the grocery store. Both can be used interchangeably in recipes. Select spheres that are heavy for their size with firmly packed, fresh-looking leaves.

Jelly-Glazed Carrots

6 servings

prep: 5 minutes   cook: 14 minutes

1   (2-pound) package baby carrots
1   (10½-ounce) can condensed chicken
        broth, undiluted

2   tablespoons butter
1   (10½-ounce) jar red hot pepper jelly

1 Combine carrots and chicken broth in a large skillet over medium-high heat. Bring to a boil, and cook, stirring often, 6 to 8 minutes or until carrots are crisp-tender.

2 Stir in butter and jelly, and cook, stirring constantly, 5 minutes or until mixture thickens and glazes carrots.

We used hot pepper jelly to give these carrots an extra boost of flavor. Keep a couple of jars on hand—it's great over cream cheese, too, when you need an appetizer in a hurry!

Chili Corn on the Cob

4 servings

prep: 15 minutes   cook: 7 minutes

¼   cup butter, softened
1   tablespoon chopped fresh chives or
        1 teaspoon dried chives
1   teaspoon chili powder

4   ears fresh corn, husks removed

¼   teaspoon salt
¼   teaspoon pepper

1 Stir together butter, chives, and chili powder; set aside.

2 Wrap each ear of corn loosely in plastic wrap; arrange, with narrow ends in center, on a glass plate.

3 Microwave at HIGH 7 minutes, turning corn after 3½ minutes. Let stand 2 minutes. Remove plastic wrap; brush with butter mixture. Sprinkle with salt and pepper.

Corn Crop

Peak season for fresh corn is May through September. When buying fresh corn, look for bright green, snug husks; golden brown silks; and plump, milky kernels. It's best cooked and served the day it's purchased. We recommend storing it in the refrigerator no more than 2 days, and don't remove the husks until right before cooking.

Creamy Cucumber Salad

6 servings

prep: 10 minutes

1 cup plain yogurt
2 cloves garlic, minced
1 tablespoon dried mint
1 tablespoon dried parsley
½ teaspoon salt
¼ teaspoon pepper
4 cucumbers, peeled, seeded, and
    thinly sliced (see tip)

1 Stir together first 6 ingredients. Add cucumbers, and toss.

Fancy Schmancy Cucumbers

For a decorative touch, leave the cucumbers unpeeled. Pull the tines of a fork down the length of each cucumber, and then slice as directed.

Sassy Mushrooms 'n' Peas

4 servings

prep: 5 minutes   cook: 15 minutes

2   tablespoons butter
2   tablespoons grated onion
2   cloves garlic, pressed
1   (8-ounce) package sliced fresh
     mushrooms
1   (10-ounce) package frozen green
     peas
½   teaspoon chopped fresh or dried
     rosemary (see tip)
¼   teaspoon ground nutmeg
¼   teaspoon salt
¼   teaspoon pepper

1 Melt butter in a large skillet over medium heat; add onion, garlic, and mushrooms, and sauté 3 to 4 minutes or until liquid evaporates. Stir in peas and remaining ingredients; cover and cook 4 minutes. Stir and cook, uncovered, 4 more minutes or until thoroughly heated.

Fresh or Dried?

Fresh rosemary has a stronger flavor than dried; however, use equal amounts when substituting dried for fresh. Other dried herbs have a more concentrated flavor, so you'll want to use a third less of dried than fresh.

Simple Stir-fried Okra

4 to 6 servings

prep: 10 minutes   cook: 20 minutes

2   tablespoons vegetable oil
1   medium-sized sweet onion,
        chopped
1   teaspoon mustard seeds (see tip)
½   teaspoon ground cumin
¼   teaspoon crushed red pepper

1   (16-ounce) package frozen okra,
        thawed, or 1 pound fresh okra
¾   teaspoon salt

1 Heat oil in a large skillet over medium-high heat. Add onion and next 3 ingredients, and sauté 5 minutes or until onion is tender.

2 Add okra; sauté 15 minutes or until okra is light golden. Stir in salt.

"Don't have mustard seeds on hand? Just substitute ½ teaspoon dry mustard for 1 teaspoon mustard seeds."

Green Peas with Bacon

6 servings

prep: 12 minutes   cook: 18 minutes

2   slices smoked bacon

1   shallot, sliced (see note)
½   teaspoon grated orange rind
½   cup orange juice
¼   teaspoon salt
½   teaspoon pepper
1   (16-ounce) bag frozen green peas,
        thawed (see tip)
1   teaspoon butter
1   tablespoon chopped fresh mint or
        1 teaspoon dried mint

1 Cook bacon in a medium skillet until crisp; remove and drain on paper towels, reserving 1 teaspoon drippings in skillet. Crumble bacon, and set aside.

2 Sauté shallot in hot bacon drippings over medium-high heat 2 minutes or until tender. Stir in orange rind, orange juice, salt, and pepper. Cook, stirring occasionally, 5 minutes or until reduced by half. Add peas, and cook 5 more minutes; stir in butter and mint.

3 Transfer peas to a serving dish, and sprinkle with crumbled bacon.

Note: Two tablespoons chopped onion plus 1 tablespoon chopped garlic can be substituted for the shallot.

Perfect Peas

If you have extra time, buy fresh green peas in the spring when they're in season. Most farmers markets have already-shelled peas for sale—a big time-saver! Substitute 3 cups shelled fresh green peas for the 16-ounce bag of frozen green peas. Cook peas in boiling water 5 minutes, and proceed with the recipe.

Pineapple Bake

8 servings

prep: 5 minutes   cook: 25 minutes

2   (20-ounce) cans sliced pineapple in
        juice, undrained
2   cups (8 ounces) shredded sharp
        Cheddar cheese

²⁄₃   cup sugar
¹⁄₃   cup all-purpose flour
1   cup round buttery cracker crumbs
        (about 33 crackers)
¹⁄₄   cup butter, melted

1 Preheat the oven to 350°. Drain sliced pineapple, reserving ¹⁄₃ cup juice. Place pineapple in a lightly greased 7" x 11" baking dish; sprinkle with cheese.

2 Combine reserved pineapple juice, sugar, and flour; pour over cheese. Combine cracker crumbs and butter, and sprinkle over flour mixture.

3 Bake at 350° for 25 minutes or until bubbly.

❝Lookin' for something different to serve with your entrées? Try this easy side dish. It goes great with ham, pork, chicken, or turkey.❞

Speedy Garlic Mashed Potatoes

(pictured on page 105)

4 to 6 servings

prep: 5 minutes   cook: 13 minutes

1   (22-ounce) package frozen mashed
      potatoes
2⅓ cups milk

1   (4-ounce) container garlic-and-herb
      spreadable cheese (see tip)
½   teaspoon salt
½   teaspoon pepper

1 Stir together frozen potatoes and
milk in a large microwave-safe bowl.
Microwave, covered, at HIGH 10 minutes.

2 Stir in cheese, salt, and pepper.
Microwave at HIGH 3 more minutes
or until cheese melts and mixture is thoroughly heated. Serve immediately.

Say "Cheese"!

If you can't find garlic-and-herb spreadable cheese,
make your own by combining 1 (3-ounce) package
cream cheese, softened and cubed; 3 tablespoons
butter; 1 minced clove of garlic; and ½ teaspoon
of your favorite herb.

Praline Sweet Potatoes

4 servings

prep: 10 minutes   cook: 25 minutes

¼   cup butter
2½   pounds sweet potatoes, peeled and
        cut into ¼" slices

¼   cup granulated sugar
¼   cup packed light brown sugar
¼   cup pecans, chopped
¼   teaspoon ground cinnamon
⅛   teaspoon salt
2   tablespoons water

1 Melt butter in a large skillet over medium heat. Add sweet potatoes; cover and cook 10 minutes or until golden. Flip potato slices; cover and cook 10 more minutes.

2 Add sugars and next 3 ingredients to skillet, tossing to coat. Add water, stirring to loosen particles from bottom of skillet. Cook 5 minutes or until potatoes are glazed and tender.

This dish is so sweet, you'll wonder if you're eating dessert! It's a great choice with ham or turkey. And who says you can't eat dessert first?!

Tomato-Spinach Sauté

3 servings

prep: 10 minutes   cook: 5 minutes

1   tablespoon olive oil
1   (10-ounce) package fresh spinach
½   teaspoon salt, divided
½   teaspoon coarsely ground pepper,
        divided

2   cloves garlic, minced
1   medium-sized tomato, chopped
1   tablespoon balsamic vinegar
        (optional)
Salt to taste (optional)

1 Heat oil in a nonstick skillet over medium-high heat. Sauté spinach 2 minutes or until wilted. Stir in ¼ teaspoon each of salt and pepper. Transfer to a serving platter.

2 Add garlic to skillet, and sauté 1 minute. Stir in chopped tomato, and sauté until thoroughly heated. Stir in remaining ¼ teaspoon each of salt and pepper. Spoon mixture over spinach on platter. Drizzle with vinegar, if desired, and serve immediately. Lightly salt to taste, if desired.

"Popeye was right—spinach makes you strong! Plus it's a good source of fiber and calcium. In this recipe, it's sautéed with fresh garlic, which is believed to help control blood pressure and lower the risk of cancer. So eat up!"

Zucchini Medley

10 to 12 servings

prep: 10 minutes   cook: 26 minutes

4	medium-sized zucchini
¼	cup vegetable oil
1	small onion, chopped
1	(8-ounce) can roasted garlic tomato sauce
2	white bread slices
1	cup (4 ounces) shredded sharp Cheddar cheese
½	teaspoon salt
¼	cup grated Parmesan cheese

1 Preheat the oven to 350°. Cut zucchini in half lengthwise; cut halves crosswise into ¼"-thick slices.

2 Heat oil in a Dutch oven over medium-high heat. Sauté zucchini and onion in hot oil until tender. Combine zucchini mixture, tomato sauce, and next 3 ingredients.

3 Spoon mixture into a lightly greased 7" x 11" baking dish; sprinkle with Parmesan cheese. Bake at 350° for 18 minutes or until bubbly.

❝*If you're not counting calories, top this with some cooked crumbled bacon. It's a nice finish for this tasty vegetable medley.***❞**

Journey Cakes

20 cakes

prep: 5 minutes   cook: 4 minutes per batch

2   cups cold, cooked basmati or
        long-grain rice
2   large eggs, lightly beaten
2   cups milk
2   cups all-purpose flour
1½ tablespoons butter, melted
2   teaspoons salt

Peanut oil

1 Stir together all ingredients except oil in a large bowl.

2 Pour oil to a depth of ¼" into a large heavy skillet; heat to 350°.

3 Drop batter by ¼-cupfuls into hot oil; fry cakes, in batches, 2 minutes on each side or until golden. Drain on wire racks over paper towels. Serve immediately.

Food to Go
Journey cakes are thought to be an early version of road food. Field workers and travelers would tuck several cakes into their pockets for a simple meal on-the-go.

Cranberry-Orange Couscous

4 to 6 servings

prep: 25 minutes

1   teaspoon grated orange rind
2   cups orange juice
⅓   cup sweetened dried cranberries
½   tablespoon butter
1   teaspoon minced fresh ginger or
      a pinch of ground ginger
½   teaspoon salt
¼   teaspoon ground cinnamon

1   (10-ounce) package couscous
¼   cup sliced almonds, toasted
      (see tip on page 134)

1 Bring first 7 ingredients to a boil in a saucepan over medium heat; remove from heat.

2 Stir in couscous. Cover and let stand 5 minutes. Fluff with a fork; stir in almonds.

"Haven't tried couscous because of its exotic-sounding name? Don't be misled—it's actually a tiny pasta made from semolina wheat. And if you like rice, you'll like couscous."

Green-and-Gold Salad with Citrus Ranch Dressing

4 to 6 servings

prep: 25 minutes

¾ cup buttermilk Ranch-style dressing
2 teaspoons grated orange rind
3 tablespoons orange juice

3 cups chopped fresh broccoli
1½ cups diced mango
1 large navel orange, sectioned and chopped
½ cup pecans, toasted (see tip on page 134)
1 (6-ounce) package fresh baby spinach

1 Stir together first 3 ingredients in a small bowl; cover and chill until ready to serve.

2 Combine broccoli and remaining 4 ingredients in a large bowl. Add dressing; toss to coat.

Refrigerated fruit slices will save you a lot of time on prep. And if you opt to squeeze your own orange juice, grate your rind first, then squeeze.

Italian Bread Salad

8 servings

prep: 25 minutes

¼ cup balsamic vinegar
2 tablespoons olive oil
¼ teaspoon salt
¼ teaspoon pepper

10 (1"-thick) stale Italian bread slices,
  cut into 1" cubes
6 plum tomatoes, chopped
1 small red onion, chopped
¼ cup chopped fresh basil or
  1 teaspoon dried basil
¼ cup chopped fresh oregano or
  1 teaspoon dried oregano

1 Whisk together first 4 ingredients in a small bowl until well blended.

2 Combine bread cubes and remaining 4 ingredients in a large bowl. Add dressing; toss gently. Let stand 20 minutes before serving.

Plan Ahead
Once you've tossed the salad, letting it stand for 20 minutes gives all the flavors a good chance to "marry."

Fuss-Free Breads

66Mere minutes is all it takes to fill your home with the aroma and goodness of these freshly baked breads.99

Almond Bear Claws

1 ½ dozen

prep: 18 minutes   cook: 18 minutes

1   (17.3-ounce) package frozen puff
       pastry sheets, thawed
1   (12-ounce) can almond filling

1   egg yolk
2   tablespoons water
⅓   cup sliced almonds

1   cup semisweet chocolate chips

1 Preheat the oven to 400°. Cut each puff pastry sheet into 9 (3") squares. Spread half of each square with 2 teaspoons almond filling. Fold top half of pastry over filling, pressing edges gently to seal. Using a sharp knife, cut 3 slits in top of pastry; curve pastry slightly to resemble claws, and place on lightly greased baking sheets.

2 Whisk together egg yolk and water in a small bowl; brush egg mixture over pastries, and sprinkle evenly with almonds.

3 Bake at 400° for 16 minutes or until golden. Remove from pans to a wire rack; cool.

4 Microwave chocolate chips in a small bowl at MEDIUM (50% power) 1 ½ minutes or until chocolate melts, stirring halfway. Drizzle chocolate evenly over pastries.

"With the slits cut on top, these pastries resemble a bear's claw. And you'll need a bear-sized appetite to wolf down these treats—ooh they're so good!!"

Pumpkin Doughnut Holes

2 dozen

prep: 8 minutes   cook: 28 minutes

Vegetable oil

1   cup self-rising flour
¾   cup canned pumpkin
¼   cup packed brown sugar
1   large egg, lightly beaten
1   teaspoon grated orange rind
1   teaspoon ground cinnamon
¼   teaspoon ground nutmeg

Powdered sugar

1 Pour oil to a depth of 1½" in a Dutch oven; heat to 365°.

2 Meanwhile, combine flour and next 6 ingredients in a large bowl.

3 Drop pumpkin batter by level tablespoonfuls into hot oil; fry doughnut holes, a few at a time, 2 minutes or until golden, turning at least once. Drain on paper towels. Roll doughnut holes in powdered sugar; serve warm.

"The flavors of fall are mixed together in these tasty doughnut holes. You can enjoy them year-round with the convenience of canned pumpkin. Plus, my version is much easier than traditional doughnut holes. Just drop the batter by tablespoonfuls and fry like fritters."

Super-Easy Beignets

2 dozen

prep: 24 minutes   cook: 24 minutes   other: 12 hours

1   (32-ounce) package frozen bread
      dough loaves

Vegetable oil
Powdered sugar

1 Place both frozen bread dough loaves on a greased baking sheet. Cover loosely with a clean damp towel, and cover towel loosely with a sheet of plastic wrap. Let dough thaw and rise, covered, in the refrigerator overnight.

2 Transfer dough to a lightly floured surface; cover and let stand at room temperature 30 minutes. Using a serrated knife, cut each loaf into 12 equal pieces. Cover pieces with a towel.

3 Pour oil to a depth of 2" in a Dutch oven; heat to 375°. Fry dough, 4 pieces at a time, 1 to 2 minutes on each side or until golden; drain on paper towels. Roll warm beignets in powdered sugar. Serve immediately.

❝Experience a taste of the Big Easy with my Super-Easy Beignets. Don't skimp on the powdered sugar—it's a must!❞

Parmesan Dinner Rolls

16 rolls

prep: 11 minutes   cook: 27 minutes

2¼ cups biscuit baking mix, divided
½   cup grated Parmesan cheese
1   (8-ounce) container sour cream
½   cup butter, melted
½   teaspoon ground black pepper

1 Preheat the oven to 350°. Combine 2 cups biscuit mix and the remaining 4 ingredients in a large bowl; stir just until dry ingredients are moistened.

2 Sprinkle remaining ¼ cup biscuit mix onto work surface. Drop dough evenly onto work surface in 16 portions; roll each portion into a ball. Place balls into lightly greased muffin pans.

3 Bake at 350° for 24 to 27 minutes or until lightly browned. Let cool in pans 1 minute. Serve warm.

"Biscuit baking mix is my secret to providing these melt-in-your mouth rolls for your family supper tonight."

Herbed Focaccia

8 servings

prep: 5 minutes   cook: 10 minutes

1   (11-ounce) can refrigerated French bread dough (see tip)
2   tablespoons olive oil
1   teaspoon kosher salt
1   teaspoon ground pepper
1   teaspoon dried oregano
1   teaspoon dried basil
½   teaspoon dried thyme

1 Preheat the oven to 375°. Unroll dough into a 10" x 15" greased rimmed baking pan, and flatten slightly. Press handle of a wooden spoon into dough to make indentations at 1" intervals; drizzle dough with oil, and sprinkle with salt and remaining ingredients.

2 Bake at 375° for 10 minutes or until lightly browned. Cut bread into rectangles, and serve warm.

Head Start

Refrigerated French bread dough gives you a jump start on this crispy, crunchy focaccia. Serve it plain, with warm marinara sauce, or crowned with your favorite pizza toppings.

Cheesy French Bread

8 servings

prep: 5 minutes   cook: 5 minutes

1   (16-ounce) French bread loaf
¼   cup Italian dressing
¼   cup (1 ounce) shredded Italian
        cheese blend
1½   tablespoons minced fresh basil or
        2 teaspoons dried basil

1 Preheat the broiler. Cut bread into 1"-thick slices, and place on a baking sheet. Brush with dressing, and sprinkle with cheese and basil.

2 Broil 5½" from heat until cheese melts. Serve immediately.

66Serve the gang this quick-and-easy bread for a nice change from garlic bread.99

Buttery Garlic Bread

8 servings

prep: 5 minutes   cook: 7 minutes

½   cup butter
4   cloves garlic, pressed
½   teaspoon salt

1   (16-ounce) Italian bread loaf

¼   cup grated Parmesan cheese
1½   teaspoons dried Italian seasoning

1 Preheat the broiler. Melt butter in a skillet over medium-high heat; add garlic and salt, and sauté 2 minutes.

2 Cut bread into 1½" slices, and dip into butter mixture, coating both sides. Place on a baking sheet.

3 Stir together Parmesan cheese and Italian seasoning; sprinkle on each bread slice.

4 Broil 5½" from heat 4 minutes or until cheese melts.

66*Sliced Italian bread dipped in a buttery garlic mixture, sprinkled with Parmesan cheese, and popped in the broiler?! Yum-my! It's great with Zesty Spaghetti and Meatballs on page 10.*99

Tomato-Cheese Bread

6 servings

prep: 8 minutes   cook: 5 minutes

1   (8-ounce) container soft cream
     cheese

¼ cup shredded Parmesan cheese

1   clove garlic, pressed

2   tablespoons chopped fresh basil or
     2 teaspoons dried basil

¼ teaspoon salt

⅛ teaspoon pepper

1   (16-ounce) French bread loaf

2   plum tomatoes, sliced

1 Preheat the broiler. In a 1-quart microwave-safe bowl, microwave cream cheese at HIGH 20 seconds. Stir in Parmesan cheese and next 4 ingredients.

2 Cut bread in half lengthwise; spread cream cheese mixture over cut sides of bread. Top with tomatoes. Place on a baking sheet, cut side up.

3 Broil 5½" from heat 4 to 5 minutes. Slice and serve.

Plum Tomatoes

Because they're a little less juicy but always pretty and yummy, plum tomatoes are the tomato of choice atop this cheesy French bread loaf. Consider using them whenever vine-ripe tomatoes are out of season. You'll get quality flavor and texture—even during the winter months.

Crispy Breadsticks

2 dozen

prep: 10 minutes   cook: 10 minutes

½   cup olive oil
2   cloves garlic, minced
1   tablespoon chopped fresh parsley or
        1 teaspoon dried parsley
1   tablespoon chopped fresh or dried
        rosemary
¼   teaspoon salt
¼   teaspoon coarsely ground pepper
2   (6-ounce) French bread loaves,
        halved lengthwise
¼   cup shredded Parmesan cheese

1 Preheat the oven to 425°. Combine first 6 ingredients. Cut bread halves into ½" slices. Place on baking sheets. Brush with oil mixture, and sprinkle with cheese.

2 Bake at 425° for 7 to 10 minutes or until cheese melts.

These bite-sized breadsticks may never make it to your dinner table if you start snacking when they come out of the oven. Better double the recipe!

Spiced Croutons

4 cups

prep: 5 minutes   cook: 15 minutes

½ (8-ounce) French bread loaf, cubed
Nonstick cooking spray
¼ teaspoon apple pie spice

1 Preheat the oven to 375°. Coat bread cubes evenly with nonstick cooking spray. Place in a resealable plastic bag; add spice. Seal bag, and shake to coat. Arrange bread cubes on a baking sheet.

2 Bake at 375° for 10 to 15 minutes or until browned. Cool.

The Crunch on Croutons

Flavored with apple pie spice, these croutons lend a nice crunch to warm autumn soups and winter fruit salads.

Crusty Cornbread

6 servings

prep: 10 minutes   cook: 25 minutes

¼   cup butter

2   cups self-rising buttermilk white
        cornmeal mix
½   cup all-purpose flour

2   cups buttermilk
1   large egg

1 Preheat the oven to 450°. Place butter in a 9" cast-iron skillet, and heat 5 minutes or until melted.

2 Combine cornmeal mix and flour in a large bowl.

3 Stir together buttermilk and egg. Add to dry ingredients; stir just until moistened. Pour over melted butter in skillet.

4 Bake at 450° for 20 minutes or until golden. Cut into wedges, and serve.

Golden Goodness

Pouring the batter into melted butter in a hot cast-iron skillet jump-starts the nice and golden crust on this cornbread that lends down-home comfort to a bowl of soup or practically any dinner.

Sweet Onion Cornbread

9 servings

prep: 15 minutes   cook: 25 minutes

1   medium-sized sweet onion,
        chopped
Nonstick cooking spray

1   (8-ounce) package corn muffin mix
½   cup sour cream
½   cup (2 ounces) shredded Cheddar
        cheese

1 Preheat the oven to 400°. Sauté chopped onion in a small skillet coated with nonstick cooking spray until tender.

2 Prepare corn muffin batter according to package directions; pour into a lightly greased 8" square pan, and top with onion. Stir together sour cream and cheese; spread over onion.

3 Bake at 400° for 25 minutes or until golden. Let stand 10 minutes before cutting into squares.

Cornbread doesn't require rising time, so you can serve up this old-time favorite with minimal work.

Sausage-and-Cheddar Muffins

1 dozen

prep: 15 minutes   cook: 23 minutes

3   tablespoons butter
1   medium-sized sweet onion, finely
       chopped

1 ½ cups biscuit baking mix
2   cups (8 ounces) shredded Cheddar
       cheese, divided

½   cup milk
1   large egg
½   pound hot or mild ground pork
       sausage, cooked and crumbled

1 Preheat the oven to 425°. Melt butter in a skillet over medium-high heat; add onion, and sauté 3 to 5 minutes or until tender; set aside.

2 Combine biscuit mix and 1 cup cheese in a large bowl; make a well in center of mixture.

3 Stir together milk and egg, blending well; add to cheese mixture, stirring just until moistened. Stir in onion and sausage. Spoon into lightly greased muffin pans, filling two-thirds full. Sprinkle with remaining 1 cup cheese.

4 Bake at 425° for 18 minutes or until golden. Let stand 2 to 3 minutes before removing from pans.

Mini Muffins

If you'd like, you can use this recipe to make mini muffins. Spoon batter into lightly greased miniature (1¾") muffin pans. Bake at 425° for 14 minutes or until golden. Makes 2½ dozen li'l poppers!

Cheese Muffins

1 dozen

prep: 10 minutes   cook: 20 minutes

2   tablespoons butter, divided
½   cup chopped onion

1½   cups biscuit baking mix
1   cup (4 ounces) shredded Cheddar
     cheese, divided
½   cup milk
1   large egg, beaten
1   tablespoon sesame seeds, toasted

1 Preheat the oven to 400°. Melt 1 tablespoon butter in a small skillet over medium-high heat. Add onion; sauté 3 minutes or until tender.

2 Combine onion mixture, biscuit mix, and ½ cup cheese in a medium bowl; make a well in center of mixture. In a small bowl, combine milk and egg; add to dry ingredients, stirring just until moistened. Spoon batter into greased muffin pans, filling half full. Sprinkle with remaining ½ cup cheese and the sesame seeds. Dot with remaining 1 tablespoon butter.

3 Bake at 400° for 13 minutes or until muffins are golden. Remove from pans immediately.

Peppered Cheese Muffins

For muffins with a bit of heat, substitute 1 cup of Monterey Jack cheese with peppers for the Cheddar cheese.

Pecan Mini-Muffins

40 muffins

prep: 5 minutes   cook: 12 minutes

1	cup packed brown sugar
½	cup butter, melted
2	large eggs
1	teaspoon vanilla extract
1	cup chopped pecans
½	cup all-purpose flour

1 Preheat the oven to 375°. Combine first 4 ingredients in a bowl, beating with a wire whisk until smooth. Stir in pecans and flour.

2 Spoon batter into lightly greased miniature (1¾") muffin pans, filling to within ⅛" from top.

3 Bake at 375° for 12 minutes or until lightly browned. Cool in pans on wire racks 1 minute. Remove from pans; cool completely on wire racks.

"These muffins taste like pecan tassies but are easier to prepare because there's no separate crust."

Spicy Kickin' Biscuits

1½ dozen

prep: 10 minutes   cook: 15 minutes

3½ cups biscuit baking mix
1   to 2 tablespoons taco seasoning mix
1   (10-ounce) can diced tomatoes and
     green chilies, drained
1   cup (4 ounces) shredded Monterey
     Jack cheese with peppers
1   cup milk

1 Preheat the oven to 425°. Combine biscuit mix and taco seasoning in a large bowl; add tomatoes, cheese, and milk, stirring until a soft dough forms. Drop dough by 2 tablespoonfuls onto ungreased baking sheets 2" to 3" apart.

2 Bake at 425° for 12 to 15 minutes or until biscuits are golden.

"No rollin' or shapin' needed for these golden gems. Just drop 'em by the spoonful onto baking sheets."

Jalapeño Cheese Biscuits

(pictured on facing page)

22 biscuits

prep: 14 minutes   cook: 18 minutes

½ cup butter
2 cups self-rising flour
1 cup whipping cream
¼ cup pickled jalapeño slices, chopped
½ cup (2 ounces) shredded sharp
    Cheddar cheese

1 Preheat the oven to 400°. Cut butter into flour with a pastry blender or 2 forks; stir in whipping cream just until moistened. Stir in jalapeños and cheese just until blended.

2 Turn dough out onto a lightly floured surface; knead dough 6 or 7 times. Roll or pat dough to ½" thickness. Cut with a 1½" round cutter. Place biscuits on a lightly greased baking sheet.

3 Bake at 400° for 18 minutes or until lightly browned. Serve warm.

"Have these biscuits for breakfast to jump-start your day, or you can enjoy them alongside a bowl of chili like my Very Veggie Chili on page 60."

Gingered Lemon
Cupcakes, page 183

Nutty Cranberry Popcorn,
page 203

Savory Olive and Rosemary Scones

(pictured on facing page)

8 scones

prep: 13 minutes   cook: 15 minutes

2   cups all-purpose flour
1   tablespoon baking powder
¼   teaspoon salt
1   cup grated Parmesan cheese
⅓   cup cold butter, cut into pieces
1   tablespoon chopped fresh or dried
      rosemary
⅓   cup kalamata or ripe black olives,
      chopped
¾   cup buttermilk

1½   teaspoons olive oil
¼   teaspoon freshly ground black
      pepper

1 Preheat the oven to 425°. Stir together first 4 ingredients in a bowl; cut in butter with a pastry blender or 2 forks until mixture is crumbly. Stir in rosemary and olives. Gradually add buttermilk to flour mixture, stirring with a fork just until ingredients are moistened. Turn dough out onto a lightly floured surface; knead 3 or 4 times.

2 Pat dough into an 8" circle on a lightly greased baking sheet. Cut into 8 wedges, using a sharp knife. (Do not separate wedges.) Brush with olive oil, and sprinkle with black pepper.

3 Bake at 425° for 12 to 15 minutes or until light golden. Serve warm.

Not Just for Breakfast
Black olives and rosemary flavor these savory scones. Serve them alongside your meal—especially soups or stews—or by themselves for a snack.

Blueberries and Cream Scones

8 scones

prep: 13 minutes   cook: 30 minutes

2   cups all-purpose flour
2   teaspoons baking powder
¼   teaspoon salt
⅓   cup sugar
⅓   cup cold butter, cut into pieces
¾   cup whipping cream
1½   teaspoons vanilla extract
½   cup frozen blueberries (see tip)

1   tablespoon whipping cream
1   tablespoon turbinado or granulated
     sugar

1 Preheat the oven to 425°. Combine first 4 ingredients in a bowl; cut in butter with a pastry blender or 2 forks until crumbly. Stir in ¾ cup whipping cream and the vanilla until dry ingredients are moistened. Gently fold in blueberries.

2 Turn dough out onto a lightly floured surface. Pat dough into an 8" circle on a lightly greased baking sheet. Cut into 8 wedges, using a sharp knife. (Do not separate wedges.) Brush wedges evenly with 1 tablespoon whipping cream; sprinkle with turbinado sugar.

3 Bake at 425° for 25 to 30 minutes or until golden.

Frozen Berries

Frozen blueberries are the choice for these scones. Quickly rinse off any ice crystals from the frozen berries, if desired, but do not allow them to thaw or they'll become mushy and "bleed" during baking.

Dazzling Desserts

Satisfy the gang's sweet tooth on the double with tempting treats like Double Chocolate Toffee Brownies on page 198. For more hard-to-resist desserts, just turn the page.

Candy Bar Cake

12 servings

prep: 10 minutes   cook: 28 minutes

1   (18.25-ounce) package yellow cake
     mix

1   (12.25-ounce) jar caramel topping

1   (8-ounce) package cream cheese,
     softened
½   cup creamy peanut butter
¼   cup butter, softened
2½   cups powdered sugar
1   tablespoon milk
1   teaspoon vanilla extract
4   (2.07-ounce) chocolate-coated
     caramel-peanut nougat bars,
     chopped

1 Preheat the oven to 350°. Prepare cake mix according to package directions in a lightly greased 9" x 13" baking pan. Cool completely in pan on a wire rack.

2 Gently poke holes in top of cake, using the end of a wooden spoon. Pour caramel topping slowly over cake.

3 Beat cream cheese, peanut butter, and butter at medium speed of an electric beater until creamy. Gradually add powdered sugar, beating at low speed until smooth; add milk. Stir in vanilla. Spread evenly over cake; sprinkle with chopped candy bars. Cover and chill until ready to serve. Cut into squares.

❝You'd never guess that this cake started with a mix. It's dressed up with a layer of caramel topping and topped with peanut butter frosting. But it's not finished until chopped candy bars are sprinkled on top!❞

Pineapple-Coconut Cake

12 servings

prep: 20 minutes   cook: 28 minutes   chill: 9 hours

1 (3.4-ounce) package French vanilla instant pudding mix

1 (18.25-ounce) package white cake mix

1 (20-ounce) can crushed pineapple, well drained

1 cup sweetened flaked coconut

1 cup chopped pecans or macadamia nuts, toasted (see tip on page 134)

1 (8-ounce) container frozen whipped topping, thawed

1 Preheat the oven to 350°. Prepare pudding according to package directions; chill 1 hour.

2 Meanwhile, prepare cake mix according to package directions in a 9" x 13" baking pan. Cool completely in pan on a wire rack.

3 Spread chilled pudding over cake. Spoon pineapple over pudding. Sprinkle with coconut and half of pecans. Spread with whipped topping, and sprinkle with remaining half of pecans. Cover and chill 8 hours. Cut into squares.

Start with a Mix

Instant pudding mix, cake mix, and other convenience ingredients shorten this recipe's prep and bake times but don't compromise on flavor.

Pineapple Right-Side-Up Cake

12 servings

prep: 8 minutes   cook: 30 minutes

1   (8-ounce) can crushed pineapple,
        undrained

2½   cups all-purpose flour
1   tablespoon baking powder
¼   teaspoon salt
¾   cup granulated sugar

⅓   cup milk
⅓   cup butter, melted
2   large eggs, lightly beaten
½   teaspoon vanilla extract
⅓   cup packed brown sugar

1 Preheat the oven to 350°. Drain pineapple, reserving ⅓ cup juice; set both aside.

2 Combine flour and next 3 ingredients; make a well in center.

3 Stir together reserved pineapple juice, the milk, and next 3 ingredients; add to dry ingredients, stirring just until moistened. Spoon into a lightly greased 9" x 13" baking pan. Top with pineapple and brown sugar.

4 Bake at 350° for 25 to 30 minutes or until a wooden toothpick inserted in center comes out clean. Cool in pan on a wire rack. Cut into squares.

"No need to invert the baking pan here. This pineapple cake bakes right-side up! It's an oh-so-sweet ending sure to make any meal oh-so-special."

Gingered Lemon Cupcakes

(pictured on page 174)

2 dozen

prep: 20 minutes   cook: 22 minutes

1   (18.25-ounce) package lemon
        cake mix
1   (8-ounce) container sour cream
⅓   cup finely chopped crystallized
        ginger or ½ teaspoon ground
        ginger (see tip)

¼   cup butter, softened
1   (8-ounce) package cream cheese,
        softened
1½   cups powdered sugar
1   teaspoon grated lemon rind
1   teaspoon lemon juice
Garnish: chopped crystallized ginger

1 Preheat the oven to 350°. Prepare cake mix according to package directions. Stir in sour cream and ⅓ cup crystallized ginger. Pour batter into muffin pans lined with paper liners, filling two-thirds full.

2 Bake at 350° for 22 minutes or until a wooden toothpick inserted in center comes out clean. Remove from pans, and cool completely on a wire rack.

3 Meanwhile, beat butter and cream cheese at medium speed of an electric beater until smooth. Gradually add powdered sugar, beating at low speed until light and fluffy. Stir in rind and juice. Spread frosting generously over cupcakes. Garnish, if desired.

❝My gang loves the subtle flavor and crunch of the crystallized ginger in these cupcakes. Look for it in the spice section of your supermarket. If you can't find crystallized, then substitute ground—but remember that the crunch will be missing!❞

Cupcake Surprises

2 dozen

prep: 20 minutes   cook: 22 minutes

1   (18.25-ounce) package Swiss
      chocolate cake mix

2   (3-ounce) packages cream cheese,
      softened
½   cup sugar
1   large egg, lightly beaten
1   cup (6 ounces) milk chocolate chips
¼   cup sweetened flaked coconut

1 Preheat the oven to 350°. Prepare cake mix according to package directions; set batter aside.

2 Stir together cream cheese, sugar, and egg. Stir in chocolate chips and coconut.

3 Pour batter evenly into muffins pans lined with paper liners, filling half full. Drop cream cheese mixture by rounded teaspoonfuls evenly into center of batter.

4 Bake at 350° for 19 to 22 minutes or until a wooden toothpick inserted in center comes out clean. Cool in pans on a wire rack for 15 minutes. Remove from pans, and cool completely on a wire rack.

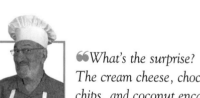

❝What's the surprise? The cream cheese, chocolate chips, and coconut encased in the chocolate cake! M-m-m!❞

Tiramisù Trifle

4 to 6 servings

prep: 20 minutes   chill: 4 hours

1	(10.75-ounce) frozen pound cake, thawed

1 Cut pound cake into 1" cubes.

1	(8-ounce) container mascarpone cheese (see note)
½	cup powdered sugar
3	cups frozen whipped topping, thawed and divided

2 Beat mascarpone cheese at medium speed of an electric beater until creamy; gradually add powdered sugar, and beat until smooth. Stir in 1 cup whipped topping.

1	cup strong brewed coffee, chilled (see tip)
6	(1.4-ounce) chocolate-covered toffee candy bars, crushed

3 Place ⅓ of cake cubes in a 2-quart trifle bowl. Pour ⅓ cup coffee over cubes. Top with ⅓ of cheese mixture and ¼ of candy bars. Repeat layers twice. Spread top layer with remaining 2 cups whipped topping and the remaining crushed candy bars. Cover and chill at least 4 hours.

Note: Mascarpone cheese is a soft and fresh triple cream dessert cheese with a fluffy texture.

Cup of Joe

Stir up a strong cup of coffee by spooning 1 tablespoon of instant coffee granules into an 8-ounce cup of hot water; mix and then chill.

Triple Cookie Ice Cream Pie

8 to 10 servings

prep: 14 minutes   cook: 10 minutes   freeze: 8 hours

1   (7.25-ounce) package butter cookies
      (about 24 cookies)
3   tablespoons butter, melted

1   quart vanilla ice cream, softened
6   chewy chocolate chip cookies,
      coarsely chopped
6   chocolate-covered graham crackers,
      coarsely chopped

1   (11.5-ounce) package double
      chocolate chips (1¾ cups)
1   tablespoon butter
½   cup whipping cream
¼   cup strong brewed coffee
1   teaspoon vanilla extract

1 Preheat the oven to 375°. Process cookies in a food processor until fine crumbs form. Add melted butter; pulse 3 times or until blended. Press crumb mixture into bottom and up sides of a 9" pie plate.

2 Bake at 375° for 8 minutes; cool completely on a wire rack.

3 Combine ice cream, chocolate chip cookies, and graham crackers in a large bowl; spoon into prepared crust. Cover and freeze 8 hours or until firm. Let stand 5 minutes before serving.

4 Just before serving, combine chocolate chips and next 3 ingredients in a medium glass bowl. Microwave at HIGH 1½ minutes or until melted, stirring twice. Add vanilla, stirring until blended and smooth. Serve sauce warm with pie.

Lickety-Split Ice Cream Pie

To make this pie's prep time even shorter, try using a premade vanilla wafer crust or chocolate sandwich cookie crust instead of making it yourself. You can also save time by using 1½ quarts of your favorite cookie chunk ice cream instead of stirrin' up your own.

Chocolate-Dipped Pistachio Ice Cream Sandwiches

10 sandwiches

prep: 9 minutes   cook: 2 minutes   freeze: 1 hour

2   pints pistachio ice cream
3   (7.2-ounce) packages white
        chocolate macadamia nut cookies

1½ cups (9 ounces) semisweet
        chocolate chips
1   tablespoon shortening

1 Using clean scissors, cut each container of ice cream down the side; remove ice cream from containers. Using a sharp knife, quickly slice each pint of ice cream, crosswise, into 5 (¼"-thick) slices. Place 1 slice of ice cream on each of 10 cookies. Top ice cream with 10 additional cookies. Place sandwiches on a rimmed baking sheet lined with wax paper. Place pan in freezer.

2 Melt chocolate and shortening in a small saucepan over low heat. Dip half of each ice cream sandwich in melted chocolate. Place on a rimmed baking sheet lined with wax paper; freeze at least 1 hour. Serve immediately, or cover and keep frozen.

Scream for Ice Cream!
Once chocolate has hardened, wrap ice cream sandwiches in plastic wrap, and store in the freezer for up to 1 month. You'll now have homemade ice cream sandwiches awaiting the gang's beck and call.

Dessert Tacos

4 servings

prep: 15 minutes   cook: 10 minutes

1	tablespoon sugar
¼	teaspoon ground cinnamon
4	(8") flour tortillas
1	tablespoon butter, melted

2	cups chocolate ice cream
2	kiwifruit, peeled and cut into strips
1	pint strawberries, sliced
1	cup frozen whipped topping, thawed

1 Preheat the oven to 350°. Combine sugar and cinnamon. Brush tortillas with melted butter; sprinkle evenly with sugar mixture.

2 Shape 4 sheets of aluminum foil into 4" balls on a baking sheet. Place tortillas, butter side down, on foil; press to resemble taco shells.

3 Bake at 350° for 10 minutes or until crisp. Cool completely on foil on baking sheet.

4 Remove tortillas; fill evenly with ice cream, kiwifruit, and strawberries. Dollop with whipped topping.

How 'bout a taco—for dessert?! These sweet shells are generously filled with chocolate ice cream, kiwifruit, strawberries, and a dollop of whipped topping. Muy bien, amigos!

New England-Style Bananas Foster

6 servings

prep: 10 minutes   cook: 5 minutes

⅓   cup maple syrup
⅓   cup dark rum
3½ cups diagonally sliced firm ripe
      bananas
⅓   cup chopped walnuts, toasted
3   cups vanilla ice cream

1 Combine syrup and rum in a large nonstick skillet; bring to a simmer over medium-low heat. Add bananas; cook 3 minutes, stirring occasionally. Add walnuts; cook 1 minute. Serve immediately over ice cream.

❝Maple syrup lends a New England flavor to this bananas Foster dessert. And careful cookin' those bananas. You don't want them turning dark or getting too soft!❞

Pineapple Sundaes

4 servings

prep: 6 minutes

1⅓ cups lemon sorbet
1 (8-ounce) can pineapple chunks in juice, drained
2 teaspoons chopped fresh mint
4 teaspoons sweetened flaked coconut
4 teaspoons sliced almonds, toasted (see tip)

1 Place ⅓ cup sorbet in each of 4 serving bowls. Top each evenly with pineapple, mint, coconut, and almonds.

Toasting Tips

Place almonds in a small dry skillet, and cook over medium heat for 1 minute or less, stirring constantly. Or go ahead and toast about ½ cup almonds, and keep them on hand for other uses. Place extra nuts in an airtight container, and refrigerate 3 to 6 months, or freeze up to a year.

Broiled Grapefruit

4 servings

prep: 10 minutes   cook: 4 minutes

3   large pink grapefruit

½   cup apricot preserves
1   tablespoon brown sugar

½   cup sweetened flaked coconut

1 Preheat the broiler. Peel, section, and seed grapefruit; place in 4 broiler-proof dessert dishes on a large baking sheet.

2 Combine preserves and sugar, stirring well; spoon over grapefruit.

3 Broil 5½" from heat 2 to 3 minutes or until bubbly.

4 Sprinkle with coconut; broil 1 more minute or until coconut is lightly toasted.

“In a hurry? Don't you worry! Save time by starting with bottled refrigerated grapefruit sections.”

Cranberry Pockets

8 servings

prep: 15 minutes   cook: 18 minutes

1	(15-ounce) package refrigerated pie crusts
1	(8-ounce) container cream cheese, softened
½	cup chopped fresh cranberries
½	cup chopped pecans
⅓	cup granulated sugar
1	teaspoon grated orange rind
2	tablespoons powdered sugar

1 Preheat the oven to 350°. Unroll pie crusts. Cut each pie crust into 4 squares, discarding scraps.

2 Combine cream cheese and next 4 ingredients; spread ¼ cup mixture onto each pastry square, leaving a ½" border. Moisten edges with water; fold pastry diagonally over filling, pressing edges to seal. Crimp edges with a fork. Place on lightly greased baking sheets.

3 Bake at 350° for 15 to 18 minutes or until golden. Sprinkle pockets with powdered sugar, and serve warm or at room temperature.

Pointers for Freezing

Unbaked pockets can be frozen in airtight containers up to 1 month. To serve, bake frozen pockets at 350° for 25 minutes or until golden, and then sprinkle with powdered sugar.

Raspberry-Cheese Buns

5 servings

prep: 10 minutes   cook: 15 minutes

1   (7-ounce) can refrigerated breadstick
    dough
2   tablespoons cream cheese, softened
2   tablespoons seedless raspberry jam
1   teaspoon sugar

1 Preheat the oven to 400°. Unroll dough (do not separate into strips). Spread cream cheese evenly over dough; spread jam evenly over cream cheese, and sprinkle with sugar.

2 Beginning at short end, roll up dough tightly, jellyroll fashion; pinch seams to seal (do not seal ends of roll). Cut roll along perforations in dough into 5 slices. Place slices, cut sides up, in lightly greased muffin pans. Bake at 400° for 15 minutes.

Hot Buns
To reheat leftover buns, microwave at HIGH for 10 to 15 seconds per bun, or wrap the buns in aluminum foil, and bake at 400° for 10 minutes.

Butter-Mint Shortbread

3 dozen

prep: 10 minutes   cook: 25 minutes

1   cup butter, softened
¾   cup powdered sugar
½   teaspoon mint extract
½   teaspoon vanilla extract
2   cups all-purpose flour

Powdered sugar for garnish

1 Preheat the oven to 325°. Beat butter and ¾ cup powdered sugar at medium speed of an electric beater until light and fluffy. Add flavorings, beating until blended. Gradually add flour, beating at low speed until blended. Press dough into an ungreased 10" x 15" rimmed baking sheet.

2 Bake at 325° for 25 minutes or until golden. Cool in pan on a wire rack 10 minutes. Cut into squares; sprinkle with powdered sugar. Remove from pan; cool completely on wire rack.

Butter's Best
When it comes to making shortbread, no butter substitutes allowed! Use the real thing to savor that indulgently buttery flavor.

Chewy Chocolate Cookies

about 20 cookies

prep: 15 minutes   cook: 20 minutes

1¼ cups butter, softened
2   cups sugar
2   large eggs
2   teaspoons vanilla extract

2   cups all-purpose flour
1   teaspoon baking soda
½   teaspoon salt
¾   cup unsweetened cocoa
1   cup chopped pecans

1 Preheat the oven to 350°. Beat butter at medium speed of an electric beater until creamy; gradually add sugar, beating well. Add eggs and vanilla, beating until well blended.

2 Combine flour and next 3 ingredients; gradually add to butter mixture, beating at low speed after each addition until blended. Stir in pecans. Shape dough into 1½" balls, and place on lightly greased baking sheets.

3 Bake at 350° for 18 to 20 minutes or until lightly browned. Cool in pan 1 minute; remove to wire racks to cool.

Second Time Around

Turn these oversized cookies into ice cream sandwiches by spreading ¼ cup softened vanilla ice cream between them when cooled. Wrap individually, and freeze until firm.

Quick Peanut Butter Cookies

about 3 dozen

prep: 10 minutes   cook: 10 minutes per batch

1½ cups powdered sugar
1   cup creamy peanut butter
1   large egg
1   teaspoon vanilla extract

1 Preheat the oven to 325°. Combine all ingredients in a large bowl, stirring well.

2 Roll cookie dough into ¾" balls, and place on lightly greased baking sheets. Lightly press cookies with a fork.

3 Bake at 325° for 10 minutes. Let cool 2 minutes on baking sheets; remove to wire racks to cool completely.

"Don't slice and bake when you can stir, roll, and press just as easily! These homemade cookies will be the hands-down winner with your family!"

Jammin' Oatmeal Bars

4 dozen

prep: 11 minutes   cook: 30 minutes

2   (18-ounce) packages refrigerated
    ready-to-bake oatmeal-raisin
    cookie dough

2   (10-ounce) jars seedless strawberry
    preserves

Powdered sugar for garnish

1 Preheat the oven to 350°. Press
1½ packages cookie dough (18 cookies) evenly into an ungreased 10" x 15"
rimmed baking sheet.

2 Place preserves in a small bowl; stir
until smooth. Spread preserves over
cookie dough, leaving a ¼" border
around edges. Crumble remaining
½ package cookie dough (6 cookies)
over preserves.

3 Bake at 350° for 30 minutes or until
edges are golden. Cool completely
on a wire rack. Cut into bars. Sprinkle
with powdered sugar before serving.

*❝With just 3 ingredients, you can whip these
up in a jiffy! They make great afternoon
snacks—perfect for when your gang gets home
from school!❞*

Double Chocolate Toffee Brownies

(pictured on page 4)

2 dozen

Prep: 8 minutes   cook: 29 minutes

1	(21-ounce) package chewy fudge brownie mix
1	(11.5-ounce) package double chocolate chips (about 1¾ cups)
1	teaspoon instant coffee granules
¾	cup toffee bits, divided
½	cup semisweet mini chocolate chips

1 Preheat the oven to 350°. Prepare brownie mix according to package directions; stir in double chocolate chips and coffee granules. Pour brownie mixture into a lightly greased 9" x 13" baking pan. Sprinkle with ½ cup toffee bits.

2 Bake at 350° for 27 to 29 minutes or just until brownies pull away from sides of pan. Remove from oven; immediately sprinkle with remaining ¼ cup toffee bits and the ½ cup semisweet mini chocolate chips. Cool completely in pan on a wire rack; cut into squares.

Chocolate lovers, beware! You get a double whammy of chocolate—and a jolt of java—in every bite of these toffee brownies!

Peanut Butter Blonde Brownies

2 dozen

prep: 8 minutes   cook: 30 minutes

1   (16-ounce) package light brown
       sugar
¾   cup butter

3   large eggs
2¾ cups self-rising flour
1   (11-ounce) package peanut butter
       and chocolate chips
1   cup chopped pecans, toasted
2   teaspoons vanilla extract

24 miniature peanut butter cups,
       unwrapped

1 Preheat the oven to 350°. Heat sugar and butter together in a large saucepan over medium heat until butter melts and mixture is smooth. Remove from heat; cool slightly.

2 Add eggs, 1 at a time, beating after each addition. Add flour, stirring just until combined. Stir in chips, pecans, and vanilla. Pour into a greased 9" x 13" baking pan.

3 Bake at 350° for 28 minutes. Immediately press miniature peanut butter cups into brownies at even intervals. Cool in pan on a wire rack; cut into bars, with a peanut butter cup in center of each brownie.

Even Cut

Be sure to cut the brownies so that each bar has a peanut butter cup in the center. You don't want to miss the taste of that peanutty cup enveloped within each peanut butter-chocolate chip brownie!

Chocolate-Marshmallow Squares

2 dozen

prep: 5 minutes   cook: 4½ minutes   chill: 1 hour

1   (12-ounce) package semisweet
    chocolate chips (2 cups)
1   cup butterscotch chips
½   cup peanut butter

1   (10½-ounce) package miniature
    marshmallows
1   cup salted peanuts

1 Combine first 3 ingredients in a 3-quart microwave-safe glass bowl. Microwave at MEDIUM (50% power) 3½ to 4½ minutes or until chips soften, stirring after 2 minutes. Stir until mixture is smooth.

2 Stir in marshmallows and peanuts. Spread mixture in a lightly greased 9" x 13" baking dish. Refrigerate until firm. Cut into 2" squares. Store in the refrigerator.

Microwave Magic
Melting the candy chips and peanut butter in the microwave eliminates the hassle of a double boiler—and any chance of burning the mixture.

Candy-Covered Cherry Crunch

2 dozen treats

prep: 9 minutes   cook: 3 minutes

1	(3-ounce) package ramen noodles (see tip)
2	tablespoons butter
¾	cup chopped pistachios
1	cup coarsely chopped dried cherries
1	(16-ounce) package vanilla-flavored almond bark candy coating squares

1 Gently crush ramen noodles before opening package. Remove seasoning package; reserve for another use.

2 Melt butter in a large skillet over medium-high heat. Sauté crushed noodles, pistachios, and cherries in butter. (Be careful not to crush noodles too finely when sautéing.) Transfer noodle mixture to a large bowl to cool.

3 Melt candy coating according to package directions. Pour melted candy coating over cooled noodle mixture, tossing gently to coat. Drop candy mixture by rounded tablespoonfuls onto wax paper; let stand until firm. Store in an airtight container at room temperature.

No Seasoning, Please
Most ramen noodles come with a seasoning packet. You won't need it for this sweet treat, so save it to use as a soup base or to season veggies.

White Chocolate Salties

1 ½ pounds

prep: 10 minutes   chill: 20 minutes

1   (16-ounce) package vanilla-flavored almond bark candy coating squares

2   (3-ounce) packages salted Spanish peanuts

3   cups thin pretzel sticks

1 Melt candy coating according to package directions. Cool 2 minutes.

2 Add peanuts and pretzel sticks, and stir until coated. Drop by teaspoonfuls onto wax paper. Chill 20 minutes or until firm.

❝With its winning combination of savory and sweet, it's hard to resist this tempting treat!❞

Nutty Cranberry Popcorn

(pictured on page 175)

1 ½ pounds

prep: 5 minutes   cook: 24 minutes

6	cups popped popcorn
1	(6-ounce) package sweetened dried cranberries
1	cup pecan halves
1	cup cashews
¼	cup butter
½	cup sugar
¼	cup honey
¼	cup light corn syrup
½	teaspoon salt
¼	teaspoon baking soda
1	teaspoon vanilla extract

1 Preheat the oven to 250°. Combine first 4 ingredients in a large bowl; set aside.

2 Melt butter in a 3-quart saucepan over medium heat; stir in sugar, honey, and corn syrup. Bring to a boil, stirring constantly. Boil mixture, without stirring, 5 to 7 minutes or until mixture turns a light caramel color. Remove from heat; stir in salt, baking soda, and vanilla. Pour syrup over popcorn mixture. Working quickly, toss mixture with a wooden spoon.

3 Spoon mixture onto a lightly greased 10" x 15" rimmed baking sheet. Bake at 250° for 15 minutes, stirring every 5 minutes. Cool; break into pieces. Store in an airtight container.

❝Pop up this snack and the gang will go nuts! Try this mixture of dried cranberries, popcorn, and nuts the next time your cravings need a little sassy satisfaction.❞

METRIC EQUIVALENTS

The recipes that appear in this cookbook use the standard United States method for measuring liquid and dry or solid ingredients (teaspoons, tablespoons, and cups). The information in the following charts is provided to help cooks outside the U.S. successfully use these recipes. All equivalents are approximate.

EQUIVALENTS FOR DIFFERENT TYPES OF INGREDIENTS

A standard cup measure of a dry or solid ingredient will vary in weight depending on the type of ingredient. A standard cup of liquid is the same volume for any type of liquid. Use the following chart when converting standard cup measures to grams (weight) or milliliters (volume).

Standard Cup	Fine Powder	Grain	Granular	Liquid Solids	Liquid
	(ex. flour)	(ex. rice)	(ex. sugar)	(ex. butter)	(ex. milk)
1	140 g	150 g	190 g	200 g	240 ml
¾	105 g	113 g	143 g	150 g	180 ml
⅔	93 g	100 g	125 g	133 g	160 ml
½	70 g	75 g	95 g	100 g	120 ml
⅓	47 g	50 g	63 g	67 g	80 ml
¼	35 g	38 g	48 g	50 g	60 ml
⅛	18 g	19 g	24 g	25 g	30 ml

DRY INGREDIENTS BY WEIGHT

(To convert ounces to grams, multiply the number of ounces by 30.)

1 oz	=	¹⁄₁₆ lb	=	30 g
4 oz	=	¼ lb	=	120 g
8 oz	=	½ lb	=	240 g
12 oz	=	¾ lb	=	360 g
16 oz	=	1 lb	=	480 g

LENGTH

(To convert inches to centimeters, multiply the number of inches by 2.5.)

1 in				=	2.5 cm			
6 in	=	½ ft		=	15 cm			
12 in	=	1 ft		=	30 cm			
36 in	=	3 ft	=	1 yd	=	90 cm		
40 in				=	100 cm	=	1 meter	

LIQUID INGREDIENTS BY VOLUME

¼ tsp						=	1 ml
½ tsp						=	2 ml
1 tsp						=	5 ml
3 tsp	=	1 tbls			=	½ fl oz	=	15 ml
		2 tbls	=	⅛ cup	=	1 fl oz	=	30 ml
		4 tbls	=	¼ cup	=	2 fl oz	=	60 ml
		5⅓ tbls	=	⅓ cup	=	3 fl oz	=	80 ml
		8 tbls	=	½ cup	=	4 fl oz	=	120 ml
		10⅔ tbls	=	⅔ cup	=	5 fl oz	=	160 ml
		12 tbls	=	¾ cup	=	6 fl oz	=	180 ml
		16 tbls	=	1 cup	=	8 fl oz	=	240 ml
		1 pt	=	2 cups	=	16 fl oz	=	480 ml
		1 qt	=	4 cups	=	32 fl oz	=	960 ml
						33 fl oz	=	1000 ml = 1 liter

COOKING/OVEN TEMPERATURES

	Fahrenheit	Celsius	Gas Mark
Freeze Water	32° F	0° C	
Room Temperature	68° F	20° C	
Boil Water	212° F	100° C	
Bake	325° F	160° C	3
	350° F	180° C	4
	375° F	190° C	5
	400° F	200° C	6
	425° F	220° C	7
	450° F	230° C	8
Broil			Grill

Index

FAVORITE RECIPES

Jot down the family's and your favorite recipes here for handy-dandy, fast reference.
And don't forget to include the dishes that drew "oohs" and "aahs" when you had the gang over.

Recipe	Source/Page	Remarks